Tokens
for the
foundlings

Tokens
for the
foundlings

Edited by Tony Curtis

Foreword by Daisy Goodwin

SEREN

Seren is the book imprint of
Poetry Wales Press Ltd,
57 Nolton Street, Bridgend, Wales, CF31 3AE

Explore thirty years of fine writing at
www.serenbooks.com

First published 2012
Selection and Introduction © Tony Curtis, 2012
Poems © individual authors
Foreword © Daisy Goodwin, 2012

ISBN: 978-1-85411-581-2

A CIP record for this title is available from the British Library.

The publisher acknowledges the financial assistance of the
Welsh Books Council.
Printed by the Berforts Group Ltd, Stevenage

Cover image: Tracey Emin, 'Baby things [Mitten]', 2008, patinated bronze.
© Tracey Emin
Image courtesy Tracey Emin Studio
Collection The Foundling Museum
Photo: Chris Tribble // www.ctribble.co.uk

Royalties from the sale of *Tokens for the Foundlings* will be donated to the
Foundling Museum
www.foundlingmuseum.org.uk

CONTENTS

FAMILY ALBUM

THE MUSEUM

The Foundling Museum tells the story of the Foundling Hospital, London's first home for abandoned children, and of three major figures in British history: its campaigning founder the philanthropist Thomas Coram, the artist William Hogarth and the composer George Frideric Handel. The Museum's nationally-important collections are housed in a restored and refurbished building adjacent to the original site of the Hospital, which is now Coram Fields children's playground near Russell Square.

As well as displays and memorabilia relating to the lives of the foundlings themselves, the Museum holds the Foundling Hospital Art Collection, a remarkable Collection of eighteenth century paintings and sculptures donated by artists, which made the Hospital England's first public art gallery. The Museum is also home to the Gerald Coke Handel Collection, the largest privately-owned collection of Handel memorabilia, which reflects the Hospital's early links with the composer George Frideric Handel, who performed benefit concerts in the Hospital's Chapel.

The children's charity Coram continues Thomas Coram's pioneering work with vulnerable children and provides a living link with the original mission of the Foundling Hospital. The Museum seeks to preserve the heritage of the charity by conserving and exhibiting its historical treasures, and continuing the association with art and music through its programme of changing exhibitions, education and cultural events which complement the permanent displays. To that end it works with leading artists like Tracey Emin, Grayson Perry and Quentin Blake.

FOREWORD

There aren't many museums in London that have the power to move you to tears, but the Foundling Museum on the old Foundling Hospital site is one of them. The collection of tokens left behind by mothers who had given up their babies, is a mute, poignant testimony to the power of the bond between mother and child, a bond which is eloquently expanded in the poems set out in this book. The tokens – scraps of material, lockets, playing cards, a tiny heart shaped ring were left behind by the mothers so that they could identify their child if and when they were in a position to reclaim them. The fact that so many tokens are still in the Coram archives is an illustration of just how few of them were successful in reclaiming their lost children.

These mothers were desperate. Captain Thomas Coram opened the hospital in the eighteenth-century because, on returning to London after years spent abroad, he was horrified at the sight of babies left to die in the streets. His response was to start a 'Hospital for the Education and Maintenance of Exposed and Deserted Young Children.' It was immediately over subscribed and children had to be admitted on a lottery system; there is an etching in the Foundling Museum which shows two women getting the news about the fate of their babies, if they drew a white ball their child had a chance of a better life, a black ball could be a death sentence.

The poems in this anthology are as varied and as packed with meaning as the tokens themselves. Some of these poems are already familiar such as 'Holy Thursdays' by William Blake, others are written in response to the foundling tokens, such as 'Coram's cloth' by Tony Curtis. Perhaps the most poignant poem in the book is 'The Hidden City' which was written a mother who 'dropped' her child at the Foundling Museum in 1759; her hope and anguish push through every line. The last quatrain is heart-breaking:

If Fortune should her favours give
That I in Better plight may Live
I'd try to have my boy again
And Train him up the best of Men.

This splendid anthology is both a pleasure to read and a timely reminder of how far we have come.

Daisy Goodwin, 2012

INTRODUCTION

This anthology of writing about orphans, childhood and the family is published in support of the Foundling Museum in Bloomsbury. Every contributor has given their work so that profits from the book go to the Museum which is both an active gallery space with an historic collection, an archive of Handel manuscripts and scores and a celebration of over two centuries' work in supporting orphans and other children in need. One of the artists showing recently in the Museum was Tracey Emin and it is an image of her 'Baby Things' bronze mitten installed on one of the railings of the Museum which appears on our cover.

The Foundling Hospital was set up in 1739 by Thomas Coram, and attracted the support of Handel, Hogarth, Gainsborough, Reynolds, George II and Queen Caroline. In the following century Dickens was among its supporters. My wife Margaret and I have visited the Foundling Museum on several occasions, but the idea of doing something positive and practical to help came as a result of my association with the textile artist Rozanne Hawksley who exhibited her table piece 'Gloves for Mr Coram and Mr Handel' in the Museum from November 2011 to January 2012. I had made imaginative connections between earlier works of Rozanne's (often textiles, drawings and bones) and then written the poem 'Coram's Cloths' included in this volume. I might add that I have a personal connection with these issues because my wife's mother and her siblings were orphans at an institution in the 1920s and 1930s, the site of which has now become the Styal women's prison in Cheshire.

This anthology is organised in three sections: 'The Tender Catch' has poems concerning babies and very young children, the joy they bring and their vulnerability. The second section, 'Lost and Found Tokens' has poems about children who are orphans or who are separated from their parents. Some of these poems are a direct response to the Foundling Museum and its archive of tokens which mothers left with the babies they'd brought to the institution. This section has the only poems not of our time: there is a verse written by one of those mothers in the eighteenth century who 'dropped' her child at the Foundling Hospital hoping, in vain, to be some day reunited with him. There are also two from William Blake's poems 'The Songs of Innocence' and 'The Songs of Experience', for what celebration of childhood and its significance and of society's duty to children could exclude Blake? The third section, 'Family Album' presents a wide range of poems about family life, both from the perspective of the child and that of the parent or grandparent.

Every anthology is in a sense the indulgence of its editor. In this book I have brought together poets and poems I admire from the British Isles and the USA: some poets will be new to many readers, some are the most widely admired and lauded writers of our time. I trust that what I have collected as these Tokens for the Foundlings is a body of writing which is both moving and insightful, bringing our shared feelings about our lives and the lives of our children into fresh focus through the very special strength of poetry. I hope that Captain Coram would have appreciated the practicality of the project and Mr Handel the music in these poems.

Tony Curtis

THE TENDER CATCH

A CHILD'S SLEEP

I stood at the edge of my child's sleep
hearing her breathe;
although I could not enter there,
I could not leave.

Her sleep was a small wood,
perfumed with flowers;
dark, peaceful, sacred,
acred in hours.

And she was the spirit that lives
in the heart of such woods;
without time, without history,
wordlessly good.

I spoke her name, a pebble dropped
in the still night,
and saw her stir, both open palms
cupping their soft light;

then went to the window. The greater dark
outside the room
gazed back, maternal, wise
with its face of moon.

Carol Ann Duffy

NEW MOTHER: FIRST FEED

This gift I barely possess
Is the one clear thing I can do.
I am new and history-less
As the name on your wrist, as you.
But flesh has stored a deep kindness
Ready to welcome you.
Take it, a little silver,
Into your small purse.
There, it will gather interest –
The warm, bright weight of you.

Carol Rumens

CRYING

They cry because they're babies, babies cry –
they're hungry, uncomfortable, need to sleep
or sometimes for no reason you or I

however anxiously we empathise
can guess, or for no reason but to keep
us guessing day by day they cry and cry.

They stand up, learn to walk and talk and tie
their shoelaces. You watch them cross the street
without holding hands, but sometimes I

fall over at school, half-strangled, as they fight
for one more last goodbye and let them weep
when I am not at liberty to cry.

Their swollen soft distracted faces dry.
Mine is forgotten. Free to drag my feet
unsupervised back through the playground, I

will be late for work, but sometimes stop to spy
on them, or in a flash of childish pique
call out their names, want them to see me cry,
their fat transparent tears escape my eyes.

Kate Bingham

BABY-SITTING

I am sitting in a strange room listening
For the wrong baby. I don't love
This baby. She is sleeping a snuffly
Roseate, bubbling sleep; she is fair;
She is a perfectly acceptable child.
I am afraid of her. If she wakes
She will hate me. She will shout
Her hot midnight rage, her nose
Will stream disgustingly and the perfume
Of her breath will fail to enchant me.

To her I will represent absolute
Abandonment. For her it will be worse
Than for the lover cold in lonely
Sheets; worse than for the woman who waits
A moment to collect her dignity
Beside the bleached bone in the terminal ward.
As she rises sobbing from the monstrous land
Stretching for milk-familiar comforting,
She will find me and between us two
It will not come. It will not come.

Gillian Clarke

THE FOLD

Why would the ewes and their lambs
Assemble as though hypnotised
Around the cottage? Do they sense
A storm on its way? Or a fox?
Darkness and quiet are folding
All the sheep of Carrigskeewaun,
Their fleeces lustrous, long wool
For a baby's comfort-blanket,
For Catherine asleep in her crib
This midnight, our lambing-time.

MAISIE AT DAWN

Wordless in dawnlight
She talks to herself,
Her speech-melody
A waterlily budding.

LULLABY

The vixen will hear you cry, and the swans
On their eggless experimental nest,
And the insomniac curlew, and the leveret
That leaves a dew-path across the lawn.

Michael Longley

THOUGHTS AT THE HOUSE OF MY BIRTH

She gives me cinder tea
when I am born –
water from the well in the cellar
sweetened with a poker from the fire

kindly meant but hardly recompense
for leaving where we live
before we're born. Where?

I am forgetting as we speak
will spend my whole life
trying to remember
synapses reaching out across

my arching brain
my growing mind
a library of light.

But for now she wraps me
in a blanket lined with rabbit fur
sings to me with the coal of her voice

and I settle in to the yearning
lilt of her breast
the warming call of the embers.

Alice Allen

DAUGHTER II

Blake's angel, what makes you?
blood, bone, mineral? The black space
that creates the universe, would

if it could, suck everything in?
Sometimes
I hardly dare look, the night

losing its face to the senses
as you, with those owlish eyes,
little ribs, not long since

shocked into light
and an appetite
and your damp hair like feathers

nuzzle in beside me,
no one to answer,
or to answer to. Only

an unlearned joy when you wake
which is ours, your breath on my skin
enough to stop a heart,

to darn the threadbare morning.

Deryn Rees-Jones

NIGHT FEED

Perched on the edge of the bed, I am
marvelling in silence at our daughter
crashed out in your arms, milk-heavy, stoned
on butterfat and casein. Her quick breath
is a sheaf of smoke skittering down a field
overtaken by rain, a blurry ghost
we're still learning to call our own.

I whisper her name. She opens her eyes
to starlight on the outskirts of a town
where black hills kneel and a sclerotic owl
brings an answer to a fieldmouse's prayer.
And even as I speak, I know that she
will slip past whatever words we use
with a soft, as it were, exhalation.

Michael Murphy

from GHOSTINGS

Daughters, you were born
from the twinning of despair
and intense longing –
startling instances
of the gene that dreams
the dream of fact.

Words fly to you
daily, you are giddy
with the sound of their spinning,
you love all absurdities,
all that distorts
the mirrors of meaning.

And even now
as you learn what comes
in the guise of apples,
spindles, trolls
and gluttonous ogres,
you know what you know:

how magic works,
how the wolves and the witches
will always lose out,
and the lost slipper
never fail
to find its twin.

And the heart of the forest,
though dark, is alive
with any number
of princely riders,
their saddlebags stuffed
with ever-after kisses.

Even the word
that rhymes with breath
is no more, on your lips,

than a brief experiment
in sound, nothing
to the claims of now.

Seamless, the waking
dreams of children
in which elisions
are endless and meanings
multiple, each name
an eponym of delight:

where a handful of air
is a real gift;
a balloon, a post;
a half-bitten biscuit,
a bridge; and forever
lasts less than an hour.

But this, too,
is a dream – I sit
with a child either side
and have the view
they never will quite
have of themselves –

the head streamlined
as a cyclist's helmet,
the almost egg-like
narrowing of the skull
between back
and occipital front.

One blonde,
one brunette
and each with hair
that streams perfectly
down from the high
ridge of the crown.

Thinking of their future
admits hope
as much as fear –
it is the present
that summons their siblings,
the suffering ghost-children:

whose troubled eyes
reflect war, illness,
the lupine triumph
of adults; the forests
hushed and dead;
themselves, coffined in darkness.

Lawrence Sail

STILLBIRTH

Flesh-piece, with your gummed eyes,
numb fingertips,
who stopped swimming, who
stopped: forked out on the long cord, you were
purpled, then sunburnt
then radiantly Yemenite.

The mother, heaving at her useless
work, its limp defeat, saw the nurse's face
shut; she turned on her side, foetal,
a failing among the fertile workers
peopling the border. After all,
there were so many real deaths,

but someone wrapped you
in a prayershawl; someone
buried you among the orange trees between attacks,
and, ragged spit of humanness,
you still keep the memory bone
which will not corrupt.

Jasmine Donahaye

LIKE THE SEA

For Ffion, born 7 April 2005

What is
this tender catch,
this fresh spill of creases
and folds, small miracles of nails?

What is
this swell and heave
of laundry, old clocks struck
dumb, nights now trickling towards dawn?

And this –
your hearts adrift
from the ripple of breath
in her throat, the tug of her lips.

She's sea
flooding the plains
of your lives. Every day
it deepens – you can hardly breathe.

Lynne Rees

SEVEN ACTIVITIES
FOR A YOUNG CHILD

Turn on the tap for straight and silver water in the sink,
Cross your finger through
The sleek thread falling

– One

Spread white sandgrains on a tray,
And make clean furrows with a bent stick
To stare for a meaning

– Two

Draw some clumsy birds on yellow paper,
Confronting each other and as if to fly
Over your scribbled hill

– Three

Cut rapid holes into folded paper, look
At the unfolded pattern, look
Through the unfolded pattern

– Four

Walk on any square stone of the pavement,
Or on any crack between, as long
As it's with no one or someone

– Five

Throw up a ball to touch the truest brick
Of the red-brick wall,
Catch it with neat, cupped hand

– Six

Make up in your head a path, and name it,
Name where it will lead you,
Walk towards where it will lead you

– Seven

One, two, three, four, five, six, seven:
Take-up-the-rag-doll-quietly-and-sing-her-to-sleep.

Alan Brownjohn

TUNDRA

She was explaining how the baby
bound up by her spinning hands
was put inside the chest of her coat

how this had kept the restless
baby warm on the long journey
by train across frozen land

how the sky though beautiful
had neither watched nor cared
formal in its corridors of silver

how when she woke, the baby
wasn't there, had only ever been
a trick a slip the lining in her coat.

Alice Allen

AT TWO

We stiffen our bodies like old bones
when you plant us in buggies, high chairs,

or slip like fish from your grasp
in the retreating tides of baths. You feel

the thumps of our plump fists,
our nails ragging the tender flesh

beneath your eyes. We hide small objects
in our ears, noses, or let them lodge

in the corridors of our soft throats. We scream
when you pick us up, put us down, comb our hair,

try to measure our toes. We pinch cats, stretch
our hands into the drooling jaws of dogs.

We burn up in the early hours and practice
the art of projectile vomiting

to send you scuttling for the phone.
We hurl ourselves face first into water,

sidle through the gaps between cars and watch you
pale as we back away from you smiling.

Lynne Rees

ALL TODDLERS ARE ANARCHISTS

they take houses and shake them
leaving objects scattered
(antique and modern
their value established
by feel and rhythm)

they shred newspapers in seconds
without discrimination:
columnists of the extreme right
and extremists of moderation
are chewed into a pulpy mass

All toddlers are anarchists

they burble to dogs, cats, lamp-posts
and passing policemen
with equal lack of respect,
expecting an answer
and getting a smile
from the most glum faces

they even turn churches
into tap-dancing stages,
shops into bright mazes
and libraries into dust-blowing
glossaries of noise

All toddlers are anarchists

like Harpo Marx's scissors
they slice through
the ties of convention,
climbing over the gates
of our regulations, the first word
they utter is 'NO!'

Mike Jenkins

THE CHILD AS METAPHOR

The child pushed out the boat of his small voice
To see how far it would go. It floated free
Of him, drifting between blocks of ice.

Endangered voice on an indifferent sea
Turning its vast grey back: how would he sound
At the pole where so many had died already?

Under the ice fish screamed at newly drowned
Babies. Whales clicked their tongues and boomed
Disapproval. Creatures with teeth unbound

Their powers and terrifying voices loomed
Like buildings. It seemed the world was against him,
That any child's voice as small as his was doomed

Because there at the arctic all chances are slim
And everything, even love, freezes and disappears
Or snaps in two as the long night draws in.

So she listened to the deep voiced-child. Her ears
Were muffled against the cold but there, and there!
She heard him and she leaned down with her spears

Poised over the water. Mothers, the air
Is dangerous at the north pole. The metaphor
That is your son is crying out. Beware.

George Szirtes

SHADOW

She came. I just know she
came. At nightfall I'd place

our boy's wet things under
her pillow. Each morning

they were dry and folded.
I contrived once – to stay

awake. Saw her slow shape
cast by the moon. Saw it

pass a shoulder-bone of wall.
His cot. Those tiny fists

shadow-boxing the dark.
I called her – but had left

the key in the door so
she vanished. I can't be

sure – even now – if that
first small cry came from

the boy. Outside was all
moon and snow. And nothing

to give him. Nothing. Just
my thumb to suckle.

Mario Petrucci

EPIPHANY NIGHT

for Petra and Jonathan

Don't be afraid; it *is* fearful,
    what the out-there, the out-in-the-cold,

wants—what it whirls at us,
    its fast thick flurries in the air,

against the pane. Call it life
    arriving when least asked for. Undecided

between rain, sleet, sleet and snow,
    the gusts come, sharp as bad intent

or love. We flinch. And we open the door.

    There, where its sudden glow hits night,
they're closer than we'd guessed, these

    no-bodied shapes. Tricks of our light,
cold sparks of detail pouring through them

    out of and into the dark, they stand
as if astonished by the fact of us,

    a few specks melting on the threshold
like an offering for the child.

Philip Gross

PRINCE FELIPE PROSPERO
(1657-1661)

He wears a silver bell
so that in the shadow
of palace corridors
he can always be followed,

he wears a ball of amber
to ward off infection,
he wears an amulet
against malediction,

so blessed and protected
with hair like thistledown
and a gaze the painter
'found in heaven'.

 He wears the slightest of frowns
as if wondering
how long he must stand.

Velasquez paints him.
Death regards him
folding his arms.

Helen Dunmore

from PEARL

Then fiercer than longing came the fear.
I didn't stir or dare to call
to her: wide-eyed and silent as a hawk
in a great hall I waited there.
I knew that what I saw was spirit
and I feared for what might follow –
that within my sight she'd disappear
before I could come close to her.
So smooth, so small, so delicate,
this graceful, innocent girl now rose
before me in her royal robes,
a precious creature set with pearls.

Now, like a vision granted, showered
in a setting of jewels fit for a queen
this child as fresh as a lily-flower
stepped downward towards the stream.
The fine white linen she wore seemed woven
with light and where its sides hung open
was laced with borders of pearls far paler
and prettier than any I'd seen before.
The sleeves of her robe fell long and low,
stitched in with double rows of pearls;
her skirts of the same fine linen were trimmed
and seeded all over with precious gems.

Jane Draycott

THE
LOST AND FOUND:
TOKENS

HOLY THURSDAY

Twas on a Holy Thursday their innocent faces clean,
The children walking two & two in red & blue & green,
Grey headed beadles walked before with wands as white as snow,
Till into the high dome of Paul's they like Thames waters flow.

O what a multitude they seem'd these flowers of London town!
Seated in companies they sit with radiance all their own,
The hum of multitudes was there, but multitudes of lambs,
Thousands of little boys & girls raising their innocent hands.

Now like a mighty wind they raise to heaven the voice of song,
Or like harmonious thunderings the seats of Heaven among,
Beneath them sit the aged men, wise guardians of the poor;
Then cherish pity, lest you drive an angel from your door.

William Blake
(*from* Songs of Innocence)

THE HIDDEN CITY

Hard is my lot in deep Distress
To have no help where Most should find
Sure Nature meant her sacred Laws
Should men as strong as Women bind
Regardless he, Unable I,
To keep this Image of my Heart
'Tis vile to Murder! Hard to Starve
And death almost to me to part
If Fortune should her favours give
That I in Better plight may Live
I'd try to have my boy again
And Train him up the best of Men

*Anonymous poem written by a mother
who 'dropped' her child at the Foundling
Hospital, 1759*

CORAM'S CLOTHS

This hole cut in my dress that I worry and enlarge
with fingering is where the piece was taken
by them at the Foundlings as token
when I left my precious in their charge.

Whereby that cloth shall be the means,
they say, for me to recognise myself to her
when the world's workings and men's schemes
shall turn to mine and her favour.

Though the nights grow frost
and my fortunes tip. By then, I fear, the space
of my worrying will surely not fit
to the piece they kept, and wrote beside *Alice*.

Tony Curtis

BITYAH, PHARAOH'S DAUGHTER

No one knows her name:
parents have enough worries
without her as a role model –

single mother – *found the child in the river* –
the court sniggers. Pharaoh snarls
them into silence.

No man approaches an unclean woman –
who would want to claim that child ?
He looks too much like a Hebrew.

More than their lives' worth to say a word
other than *basket, bulrushes*,
the official line.

The boy plays around her feet,
reads, sings, is cleverer than the rest.
They clamour after him, her favourite.

Left alone and ailing, Bityah stays indoors.
He alone can humour her, make her cackle,
eat a few grapes, drink a little watered wine.

Then when he leaves she withers
never sees the bloody river,
frogs, hail, pestilence,

boils, locusts, lice, darkness
and all those babies dead.

Lynette Craig

GIRL-MOSES

From what she remembers

the set-up may as well be a pheasant,
pewter jug, chrysanthemum,
gleaming table, tight pile of plums,
a still life, not still
beneath a million Monsoon bitch-slaps –
rain painting every surface.
    Here's a taxi locked in traffic,
    a baby in a basket.

An escort from the west coast
adoption agency carries her charge
through calf-high surges
The street is their Nile,
its wet crush of noise a fast-tangled story
in an already tangled life.
    A baby in a basket,
    a taxi left behind in traffic.

She will get her to the airport,
to a family twelve time zones out.
The baby pouts.
A still life is control, inanimate.
She is not in control
on this Miriam-errand, but she will get her
    past every taxi locked in traffic,
    this baby, this basket.

Katy Giebenhain

BYE-CHILD

He was discovered in the henhouse where she had confined him. He was incapable of saying anything.

When the lamp glowed,
A yolk of light
In their black window,
The child in the outhouse
Put his eye to a chink –

Little henhouse boy,
Sharp-faced as new moons
Remembered, your photo still
Glimpsed like a rodent
On the floor of my mind.

Little moon man,
Kennelled and faithful
At the foot of the yard,
Your frail shape, luminous,
Weightless, is stirring the dust,

The cobwebs, old droppings
Under the roosts
And dry smells from scraps
She put through your trapdoor
Morning and evening.

After those footsteps, silence,
Vigils, solitudes, fasts,
Unchristened tears,
A puzzled love of the light.
But now you speak at last

With a remote mime
Of something beyond patience,
Your gaping wordless proof
Of lunar distances
travelled beyond love.

Seamus Heaney

THE SHAWL

A memory haunts me. It is the wrapping of a shawl. I am leaving the nursing home, following two women; one of them has the baby in the shawl. Snow is thick beneath our feet. It started snowing on Boxing Day and in early February it is still falling.

The women turn left – I follow. We walk up a driveway into an empty waiting room. The doctor comes to meet us, searches my face and looks at the child she delivered ten days ago. We sit on hard chairs and exchange awkward pleasantries. The baby is unwrapped from his shawl. He sleeps. I ask to hold him – here he is in my arms.

In a corner of the room near the door is a fish tank. A stream of bubbles rises slowly and continually to the surface as the colourful fish swim to and fro, to and fro. The three older women watch me with guarded glances. They do not know what I will do. 'It is time,' says one. I take the shawl, soft and woollen, and very slowly, carefully, with studied tranquillity, I wrap it around the child, before standing and handing him to one of the women. She takes him and turns, followed by the other woman, to go out of the door. I watch them go. I am one of the bubbles in the fish tank.

Mary Husted

RAIN

The day I let you go, there were floods
in Wroxeter and Bishopstown.
Leaves, caramel coloured, were swallowed
by the rivers and as weather travelled north
windows ran grey for hours.

Far from that tiny parlour room,
prams were being pushed around still dry
parks or else their thin wheels were hissing
on wide, wet paths and mothers were thinking
of feeding times, baths.

The moment of goodbye was soon over.
Woollen blanket soft between my fingers;
the silk hem of the parting dress a breath
on my skin, and your weight, like kilos of sweet
apples, swung in my arms.

And then I was cradling air and dust
and stood near the grate, in an awkward tableau
listening to rain falling into soot.
Each clear drop sent dark motes into the room
and the terrible space in my arms gathered all of them in.

Roz Goddard

STILL LIFE 1757

James, son of James Colcannon,
Late or Now of Jamaica,

The letters are scratched
on a fragment of mother of pearl –
a brief paradise lost for the girl
left behind with no name.

Qui me neglige me perd.

Next to a tiny gold ring
attached to a padlock and key,
a guardsman's brass button, filigree
charm, half a coin, a carved hazelnut shell,

You have my heart, tho' we must part

is the arm of a black wooden doll;
hanging slack on a gallery wall.

Geraldine Paine

CHILD'S MARK

Each swatch of cloth is a tongue,
a register in warp and weft, a roll
of foundling names. Here, mothers laid
their hearts on scraps: silk or wool,
splayed cards on cotton, each hand
a wager made for losing, or half a heart
rough-stitched in red then split
along its plumb, a promise kept –

though most were not. Ledgers closed,
their fabrics claimed by grime and fray.
Calico birds darken as they sing
of market bales, money owed;
linens that bellied over supple skin
wither in a breath of thyme.

Sue Rose

THE CHILDREN'S ASYLUM

The nuns are talking
but she can't understand what they say.
She feels far away, in this ward
where all the beds are tilted upright,
are too tall, are trees.
Long thin girls are sleeping in them,
wearing leaf-nightdresses,
listening to the birds in their pillows.
Her own bed is a tree,
the sheets are rough as bark.
Like a tree she has no legs, no arms.
Her dreams are breaking out of their nests,
are chicks with open beaks
and orange winglets tangled
in branches with blue echoes
that soon grow into a thick wood
around her face – a madwood
in which there are trees that are beds that are girls
that are all her.
And none of them can speak. Matron leans over
my nine-year-old mother
in a white habit woven from silence.

Pascale Petit

FAMILY BONFIRE

'Love cannot come here' – Sylvia Plath

It is closed to you now,
That place of trouble.
Those lost belongings

A bonfire of old detritus;
Antiques and heirlooms,
A faceful of flames glare through the cinders.

You are the lucky one, the love child –
Your future beyond the narrow lanes of bone
In which they have housed your abandonment.

The owls direct; wisely, the wild linnets call:
'Your time is with us now!
To this sad flesh the fit of your feathers.'

The world rolls on,
Banging its drum of travels and conquest.
Here they will come in time,
To this wind-swung aviary –

Red strawberry tree
In a grey and hopeless November;
Found key at last
To the heart's bright orphanage.

Diana Barsham

ORPHAN

May our daughters be as the polished corners
of the Temple

We knelt beside our iron beds to pray
to gentle Jesus meek and mild who held
a lamb and a lantern to comfort us:
and in assembly, in our blue serge tunics
and blazers with Masonic badges, we sang
of the Carpenter of Nazareth who stands
close by the heedless worker's side,
head bowed, showing his pierced hands
for which we, somehow, were made to feel
responsible. Just as our fathers' deaths –
when we failed to learn our logarithms –
were laid, mysteriously, at our door:
although we knew it couldn't be right
and our mothers' grieving, not our fault.

Jenny Lewis

SCHOOL DRILL

The Lower Playing Fields were out of bounds,
the bell from the Science Quad chimed seven,
small girls paraded soiled sheets with shame:
cloud shadows spread over the rounders pitch.

I wasn't chosen to be the point of the compass,
instead, a younger girl, with ramrod back, her heels
rapping over the parquet, led the formation
of wheeling girls representing the mason's art.

Orphaned children dressed in post-war drab,
utilitarian, as we were told our lives should be,
marching to *Colonel Bogey* and the *Dambusters*,
raised arms to our benefactors in dumb salutes.

Jenny Lewis

TOKENS

Objects which were left by mothers giving up their babies to the
Foundling Hospital between 1741 and 1750 and which remained
the property of the hospital governors.

1.

My heart has fled,
its good meat
a nourishment for another

and what is left
is this case for nothing,
hard and empty,

a reminder of the mother
who carried you inside her
then released you to the light.

2.

How can we be so beautiful,
rejected by our creator,
jewels born out of sand?

We grow to fit our conditions,
the mantle of our host
a temporary home.

We are firm, imperfect,
like grains of rice which do not
stave off your hunger.

Too dear for the likes of her,
your mother. A seamstress
or a lady's maid, fallen

from grace, the way we fell
from a bodice or a brooch,
our lustre dimmed.

3.

I am a shield for a thumb,
in the bright battle
of needle and thread,

an old hat, a nip of rum,
a tap on the head
for the naughty child,

a shuck of tin, a tick
on the glass from a blowse
saying 'let me in',

a neat bit, a magic trick:
tip me and I'm gone,
gone, like the girl
who handed me over,
a tiny trinket, nothing
she'd miss.

4.

I am a gaol without a door,
a will of iron. I cannot release
the circle of myself, latched

to my heartless body. No rest
from the work of obstruction,
no rest for those who've sinned.

I heave a weight, cold
to the touch, I taste of death
when you put me to your tongue

but I am speechless, charmless.
I am the warden of memory
and I have thrown away the key.

5.

This to remember her by:
her profile realised in me,
the callous ache of shell,

each curl of her hair,
the noble line of her nose,
but she remains unknown;

a speck of a woman
receding, like my nature,
underwater.

6.

to a door I cannot open
to a heart that will stay broken
to a story never told

to a Bible that holds your name
to a locket that hides your face
to the story of your shame

to a puzzle I can't mend
to a tear I can't unrend
to a story without end

Tamar Yoseloff

1. a hazelnut shell, 2. a string of seed pearls, 3. a thimble, 4. a padlock, 5. a miniature cameo, 6. a key

FOUNDLING 13287, A BOY

Speckled as a quail's egg
and regimental as braid, my cloth
was printed on a bed of nails.

Each twig on 'spriged cotten' paths an arc,
red brown and thin as drool, sprouts
exits that stop, go nowhere, belie

growth's root and fervent increase.
These slim stems might have been a map
leading to a rich, exotic

land, or the lines etched on the palm
of my hand, telling of dark
strangers and letters bearing news.

FOUNDLING 12052, A GIRL

A diamond of fitful squares flourishes a spray
of paired lines on beige cotton: each bending
toward the other to shape a bulb.

Pinned beneath: a tulip sketched in scant
outlines, fugitive marks cling to the surface
of slight paper. Burnt willow, ivory rectangle.

Her body was a cup I nestled in.
Wordless, the cup of this tulip.

Jaime Robles

LIAM: THE ADOPTED SON'S TALE

'I don't know anything about the eggs,' I said.
And it was a mercy he'd found only two empty shells
for I'd been sucking them for months.
He didn't give us food enough, my brother and I,
not for the work he made us do. And he so rich,
one field of his alone was more than nineteen acres.
So taking the eggs was easy and discreet,
I knew the hens' places better than he did,
and she would just assume a stoat had passed.
In the end it was the dog he blamed,
tying its jaws with baler twine,
weighting it with a tractor seat.
As the pond smoothed
he looked at me straight
and smiled.

Marianne Burton

BETWEEN THE DEE AND THE DON

'The middle ground is the best place to be.'
Igbo saying

I will stand not in the past or the future
not in the foreground or the background;
not as the first child or the last child.
I will stand alone in the middle ground.

I was conceived between the Dee and the Don.
I was born in the city of crag and stone.

I am not a daughter to one father.
I am not a sister to one brother.
I am light and dark.
I am father and mother.

I was conceived between the Dee and the Don.
I was born in the city of crag and stone.

I am not forgiving and I am not cruel.
I will not go against one side.
I am not wise or a fool.
I was not born yesterday.

I was conceived between the Dee and the Don;
I was born in the city of crag and stone.

Jackie Kay

THE FOUNDLING BADGE

Her raw hand reaches into the bag, feels,
grasps, reveals red, the colour of suspense;

not black, no turning for home with her basket
of shame. The wait is long.

Blood shuttles sense and changes of mind
through her head like the clank of looms.

She bites her nails deep into their quicks,
pulls her hair till her scalp bleeds.

Two women saved by white globes
prove contagious, are balled away.

Her little prince finds favour, but is snatched
before a last kiss and three things are demanded:

his name, none, lest, as her father said,
she grew too fond; his state of grace,

un-christened; and his leaving token,
a careful knot of silks, watered, lustred.

The ribbons mark him as hers, one day
she will need to remember them.

Their twins twist in her pocket; from Bloomsbury
to Spitalfields, they wind and warp her gut.

Kate Noakes

WHAT TYPESETTERS CALL THEM

Isolated lines created when paragraphs begin on the last line of a
page are known as orphans. They have no past, but they do have
a future, and they need not trouble the typographer. The stub-ends
left when paragraphs end on the first line of a page are called
widows. They have a past but not a future, and they look fore-
shortened and forlorned. It is the custom – in most, if not all the
world's typographic cultures – to give them one additional line for
company.

– Robert Bringhurst, The Elements of Typographic Style

Orphans aren't alone the way widows are alone
not the kitten heels of letters
gouging white space,
not single words riding, Huck Finn-like
on the raft of a new paragraph.

On proof, they're spared the red pen's scythe
through their x-height.

No past, but a future.

A word's position on the page
shifts with fate: kerning, line width, point size,
the sheer amount
of neighboring text. What unsettles the eye?
Who needs company?

We like orphans to be hopeful, plucky, gifted
with a clean slate,
envy their position in the world,
move steadily, vicariously forward
self-editing our futures.

Katy Geibenhain

HOLY THURSDAY

Is this a holy thing to see
In a rich and fruitful land,
Babes reduced to misery,
Fed with cold and usurous hand?

Is that trembling cry a song?
Can it be a song of joy?
And so many children poor?
It is a land of poverty!

And their sun does never shine,
And their fields are bleak & bare,
And their ways are fill'd with thorns:
It is eternal winter there.

For where-e'er the sun does shine,
And where-e'er the rain does fall,
Babe can never hunger there,
Nor poverty the mind appall.

William Blake
(from Songs of Experience*)*

FAMILY ALBUM

CHILD DRAWING IN A HOSPITAL BED

Any child can open wide
the occult doors of a colour
naively to call, 'Who's there?'
this sick girl drawing
out step invisible ones
imprisoned everywhere.
Wasp on a windowpane.

Darkest tulip her head bends,
face white as leukaemia,
till the prince in his tower,
on parole from a story,
descends by royal crayon
and, thrilled, stays half an hour.
Wasp on a windowpane.

Birds of Rhiannon, pencilled,
alight to wake the dead –
they do not sing, she rubs them out,
they smudge into vanishings,
they swoop to Nowhere
as if disturbed by a shout.
Wasp on a windowpane.

Omens. Wild astrologies whirl:
sun and moon begin to soar.
Unlikely that maroon sky
green Christmas trees fly through
– doctors know what logic's for.
tell me, what is magic for?
Wasp on a windowpane.

Now penal-black she profiles
four eerie malformed horses,
nostrils tethered to the ground.
Unperturbed, the child attends
for one to uplift its neck
and turn its death's head round.
Wasp on a windowpane.

Dannie Abse

EDVARD MUNCH: THE SICK CHILD

Disease, insanity and death were the angels
which attended my cradle.

North is a dark green sea
which the boy shaking on the bed
was born to.
                He is wrack
opening and shutting in the tide;
a ribbed shell dragged down
which waves knock
and the brine swills;

a mariner who will not drown.

                Angels
attend him into the cold:

a woman the sea has broken on
bowing her down;
a girl with red hair, face
fragile as a moon
that floats out on the dark.

Jeremy Hooker

DAY AT THE HOSPITAL

These senseless tearings,
these small red smiles, lipless
but not loveless,
have brought me back.

A dirty sock on the floor –
why make it official?

The silent drive to A+E. Mind the upholstery.
The cold corridors, wall after wall
laid out in a toothy grimace.
Bleached air, the fluorescent glare.
Bone-grey nurses looming
like Mount Rushmore in frigid winter.

The tiny paper train track
that will curl and peel at the edges –
just hand me a raspberry pie
and tell me not to eat.

Worst of all, the child,
a torso,
parked by the coke machine,
who smiles at nothing,
          his face eclipsing mine.

Crystal Jeans

THE SUNDIAL

Owain was ill today. In the night
He was delirious, shouting of lions
In the sleepless heat. Today, dry
And pale, he took a paper circle,
Laid it on the grass which held it
With curling fingers. In the still
Centre he pushed the broken bean
Stick, gathering twelve fragments
Of stone, placed them at measured
Distances. Then he crouched, slightly
Trembling with fever, calculating
The mathematics of sunshine.

He looked up, his eyes dark,
Intelligently adult as though
The wave of fever taught silence
And immobility for the first time.
Here, in his enforced rest, he found
Deliberation, and the slow finger
Of light, quieter than night lions,
More worthy of his concentration.
All day he told the time to me.
All day we felt and watched the sun
Caged in its white diurnal heat,
Pointing at us with its black stick.

Gillian Clarke

IT'S NO GOOD

I can't get the fat off my hands even though
        I'm up to my elbows in hot water that has started
        to look like milk.
                I don't want to think of detergent,
      effluent and the state of my drains.
It must be harissa that clings to my skin
            in streaks of oily scarlet.
A heavy lamb shank seemed a fine idea,
    basted with last week's Multipulciano,
        perched on a goo of onions, sugared with rosemary
                           needles.

I hate to look out from the kitchen in the evening.
        The house over there is mostly black with one
                square of light near the top.
      It's a bedroom. Her name is Clover.
    She is reading her book for
           tomorrow.
      She will turn off the nightlight herself.
When I see the whiteness of her forearm
    extend to the lamp-shade, I know
      I've never seen anyone this brave.

Rosie Shepperd

BASIC TRAINING

Spring's gamble with the primrose
and a boy's interest in hedgerows
still quick to read the weather
like a bird, even now so long after
any possible meaning, fallen
into as many ditches as the moon
and come home in the dark
but always up with the lark.
I'll tell the wide world at war
it might have done worse than
set store by priceless things.
What might be done in no one's name.

Andrew McNeillie

THE LAST BOY IN CAPTIVITY

parked, after dark,
alone but warm enough
among the boiled sweets
coated in fluff

I sleep
curled in the back seat
safe and sound
(a rug across my feet)

or breathe on the windscreen
then write my name.
When passing grown-ups stare
I do the same.

For company:
a wobbly gear-stick,
a nodding dog,
a Batman comic.

And yet it's just too dark,
in here, to read
a thing. Shadows huddle
here, and feed

while street lights light my face.
The rear-view mirror has me
wide-eyed, like a goldfish
dreaming of the sea.

Stephen Knight

ROSE PETAL SCENT

You drag the washtub onto the lawn
and fill it with fallen rose petals, floating
like little overlapping islands.

And because there aren't enough,
you pull petals from the ramblers
on the trellis – floppy yellow roses

and delicate pink roses and clusters
of deep red roses – until the inside
of the tub's velvety and sumptuous.

Then you take off shoes and socks
and step into blue zinc walls,
stamping and splashing

and running back over the grass
to fetch more petals – not caring
about the trouble you'll be in

but tearing up even tight buds,
like a fox ripping feathers
off chickens in a frenzy for blood.

You pour the cloudy brown water
into old cough mixture bottles,
and label them ROSE PETAL SCENT,

believing that by Christmas
it will smell even more wonderful
than your mother's Blue Grass,

or the frankincense the king carried
on a camel, following a star
over deserts and mountains.

Vicki Feaver

SERIOUS

Let us be serious now, says the teacher,
Inserting a pause in the hot afternoon
As she steeples her fingers and waits.

It's hard not to look at the snow
That prolongs the blue end of the day,
Not to think of it gathered

In alleys and gardens across the flat town
For a footprint, but this is Miss Garvin
And those are her fingers,

And though her long nails are a vanity
None of the sisters approves,
She speaks as they speak, for a power

That means us to answer the serious question
We have not been asked, that we cannot imagine
Or fail to be wrong in attempting:

Therefore we are serious now, as we wonder
Who might be the shameful example
To prove the unspecified point.

It may lie in the fork of a crocus
Or bury a jamjar left out on the step,
Or fall in its passion for detail

On two unburnt coals in the grate,
But the snow cannot help or survive
In the heat of the serious moment,

The void of all content
Where something, as ever, is wrong.
Across the yard the boilers roar.

Good children, we long to be serious well,
To multiply the word on slates,
To raise our voices in its name

And wear its ash with modesty.
We slip our hands behind the pipes
And turn them into gloves of pain.

Sean O'Brien

DANCING FOR MONSIEUR DEGAS

You didn't see the blisters
on my heels,
the blood in my ballet shoes,

or later, my body shaking
as I coughed
in a tenement bed,

the rented rooms where I
unlaced
to the glint of a monocle,

stroked beards browned
by tobacco
and breathed sour absinthe,

or when I slipped a wallet
in the tuck
of my skirts, the alleys

where I grazed my back
against the wall
when the top hats stayed away.

To you I was just a girl
from the opera,
a face to shape, a posture.

You tied a green ribbon
in my hair
and called me your daughter,

and though I was a dancer,
you made me
so I never moved another step.

Victor Tapner

BLOOD ALLEY

*Blood alley is the name given to a large marble, clear glass
except for a twist of red at its heart*

Your childhood token, a sickle of red in the glass, albino eye,
eye of the night-lamped hare; a perfect lob would break the
circle...

Now hold it close to the light and every fibril
seems to shred, as heart-blood hangs in water, that same dark dye,

shade of the dress she wore when you had your first full taste
of the pulp of her lip and the spittle off her tongue, the cost

to you being more than you had to give, which is why
the circle must break again and the dream unpick and the child be
lost.

David Harsent

ELEMENTARY

Like finding a river
passing over stones

in a forest – the way
the air gets mineral

and dense and fresh
and breathing feels easy

and skin senses
pleasure – so the sounds

of the schoolyard
reach me over the wall,

hover in the road,
dampen the clamour

of cars, footsteps, adult anger
and manoeuvre.

Somewhere in there
I am still running around

just as my cells
are still tight with water.

Sarah Lindon

CITEOG

There was the right way and the wrong.
Schooling meant nuns, brothers, priests,
right-handed salutes if our paths crossed.
We had to bless ourselves
passing churches, hearses, holy water fonts
with the strong hand that gripped the knife,
not the one that grasped the fork.

My brother Cathal, his first day at school,
copybook open for his baby scrawl,
clasped the yellow pencil in his left hand.
Sister Camillus stuck it firmly in his right,
threatened to strap the *citeog* behind his back
or if that didn't work, hack off the devil's paw.

Tom Lavelle

LATIN CLASS

Because it was not cold, we wondered why
Mother Assumption said to clear the aisles
and jump with oomph, in scissors girls,
before we would again read Caesar's wars.

Perhaps she hoped to jolt us from our plenty,
heart scald us to be mindful of that army,
bound by a vow to Empire, lamed
by the iron weight of their weaponry

how they climbed from tattered tents
into hazed air that smelled of oracles,
the frayed cord of their muscle stretched
tight around their star-crossed lives.

She hoped at last that we would comprehend
on the third leg of the campaign, how
they heard the death knell in their battering,
tried to read the minds of their divine.

Assumption thought the world was in translation
while we were listening only for the bell.

Siobhan Campbell

UP TO A CERTAIN AGE YOU HAVE TO COLLECT THEM

The mothers stand around the school gates
in their jumble clothes and jumpy boots.
Their children are like a squall of fresh leaves
flying fingers out.
The mothers lift on scuffed toes.
The children run on stalks.

The children shout around the school gates
their blue shirts flapping like flags.
The mothers are breathless step-aerobic
opening their arms.
The children are like a bath-water whirl
flecked with badges and bags and hurled-on coats.

The mothers are anxious like offtune radios.
Their children are soft like Azores wind.
Their noise you cannot you can you can't,
tear-gas, smell of milk and sweet sweat, thick.
This life flickers for a time, smiling,
and they want it to, then suddenly it's gone.

Peter Finch

THE MISSION ROOM

Precisely what the mission was which put
this metal church among us I don't know,
but every Friday to this hilltop hut
the children came to youth club even so.
The wind outside would shake each iron sheet.
The kind of thing that I recall today
is how the stove's warm paraffin smelled sweet –
the cabin scrapped and I long moved away.
According to the curate, seeking God
was why we met together every week,
though even now I can't but think it odd
quite how he thought the club would help us seek,
unless it's in the way my thoughts go back
to children's laughter in that iron shack.

Grahame Davies

UNDER TREES

The sun rises behind an empty red brick building.
The trees, though I don't know their names
nor geographical details of the place, take me there again
and again. The building with its modern architecture
is ordinary like my Junior High in New York.
But hooded men stalk the neighborhood.
A hundred orphans are hoarded in a single room.
The children are crying for mothers, mothers
are crying for children. The school was wired to explode.
Windows smashed. Walls demolished.
WELCOME to new students on the blackboard
next to a chair with one leg flung in a corner.

Body bags are lined up under blossoming trees.

Lynne Hjelmgaard

LATER

Passing the park gates, the child
urges his mother through.

She says "later", tries to plod on,
steering the buggy one-handed

while he wails and hauls sideways.
They must go home now

to feed the baby (wide-eyed
and oblivious). It is lunchtime:

they will have something nice.
He doesn't want it;

he wants what is passing,
the park, now, this minute.

He is young; it may be
"later" means nothing yet,

or he doesn't trust it.
There is a duck

strolling on the grass,
its green head glinting;

why should he believe
it will still be there

when they come back with bread?
If they come back.

When they go home,
he knows already,

the duck in the park
may be pushed back

behind meals, hoovering,
phone calls, behind hours

or days, although there is nothing
that matters so much,

right now, as its low chuckle,
the blue flash near its wing.

It's posing among the last
canna lilies, their edges

beginning to brown. My mother
was fond of lilies. The sun

has broken free of cloud,
for how long; the duck's head

dazzles, metallic blues
and purples in the green,

and I think the child is right
to scream as he diminishes

down the street, believing
there is no later.

Sheenagh Pugh

A GIRL CHILD HOWLS IN THE CENTRE OF JACKSON POND

balanced on a circle of sticks and mud and leaves.
A brush of wild lilac grows behind the winter barn.

Four fat-eyed women cool their toes on damp brown sand
three men scratch and squint like drunken loons
at the girl child, who screams from her nest on Jackson Pond.

She stole past the porch in a milky blue vest, round
wet rocks slipped green beneath her feet.
Her left hand held a brush of lilac from the barn.

Squares of tartan blankets spread across warm ground,
split wood shingles from the boat-house roof
float to the girl child, who cries on Jackson Pond.

Neighbours share corn rolls and cups of white clam broth.
Old dogs stretch in sleep, their faces nod like trees.
A branch of wild lilac leans against the winter barn.

There's a little round island like a heap of hollow bones
where a girl child stood howling in her vest and boots.
Silver geese swim in rings, to nest on Jackson Pond.
A brush of sweet-lilac lies curled beside the barn.

Rosie Shepperd

PICKING RASPBERRIES WITH MOWGLI

It was when he leant close to me,
his little naked torso, brown and thin,
reaching an arm into the cage
of raspberries, that I snatched a kiss.

The raspberries smelled of rosemary
and among them grew the odd sweetpea.
Do you know why they're called sweetpeas?
Mowgli asked – No, I said, why?

Because look, he said, fingering
a thin pale pod, this is the fruit
and this is the flower and inside the pod
are peas. Mowgli looked inside things.

Inside the sieve, a baby spider
trailing a thread his finger trailed
up, over, under the mounting pile
he prodded. Inside the fruit, the seed.

Don't pick the ones with the white bits,
Mowgli ordered, they taste horrid.
Sun tangled in the row of canes,
cobwebs blurred the berries. Mowgli

progressed to the apples – small
bitter windfalls. I'm going to test them,
he said, for smashes. And again,
I'm going to test them for bruises. Mowgli

throwing apples against the wall,
missing the wall, high up in the air;
Mowgli squatting, examining
for the smallest hint of decay

and chucking them if they failed the test,
healthy raspberries; Mowgli,
balancing on a rake, first thing
in the morning, grinning shyly.

Mimi Khalvati

AFTER THE EARTHQUAKE

That day, although he hadn't planned it
he wore his father's blue serge trousers
to the funeral, too long in the leg
for a fourteen-year-old. He didn't riffle
through a wardrobe of cotton twills
to lift out a tailored pair. Belt undone
like the tongue of a dead man, they were
handed up stained with rubble
and blood as he'd crouched beside
the sharp square into which they'd fitted
his father's body. Even in the photograph
his whimper is visible. But his hands aren't,
each muffled into a leg of his father's trousers.

Samantha Wynne-Rhydderch

HARBINGER

Small, polished shield-bearer
abacus of early days
and harbinger of life's happiness:

that the world offers
things scarlet and spotted
to alight, hasping and unhasping
unlikely wings;

that there can be three or thousands
but not a plague of ladybirds
no, a benediction of ladybirds
to enamel the weeds.

Small, polished shield-bearer
abacus of early days,
harbinger of life's happiness.

Helen Dunmore

THE CIRCLE

My boy is painting outer space,
and steadies his brush-tip to trace
the comets, planets, moon and sun
and all the circuitry they run

in one great heavenly design.
But when he tries to close the line
he draws around his upturned cup,
his hand shakes, and he screws it up.

The shake's as old as he is, all
(thank god) his body can recall
of that hour when, one inch from home,
we couldn't get the air to him;

And though today he's all the earth
and sky for breathing-space and breath
the whole damn troposphere can't cure
the flutter in his signature.

But, Jamie, nothing's what we meant.
The dream is taxed. We all resent
the quarter bled off by the dark
between the bowstring and the mark

and trust to Krishna or to fate
to keep our arrows halfway straight.
But the target also draws our aim –
our will and nature's are the same;

we are its living word, and not
a book it wrote and then forgot,
its fourteen-billion-year-old song
inscribed in both our right and wrong –

so even when you rage and moan
and bring your fist down like a stone
on your spoiled work and useless kit,
you just can't help but broadcast it:

look at the little avatar
of your muddy water-jar
filling with the perfect ring
singing under everything.

Don Paterson

DAYLIGHT ROBBERY

Silent as cut hair falling
and elevated by cushions
in the barber's rotating chair
this seven-year-old begins to see
a different boy in the mirror,
glances up, suspiciously,
like a painter checking for symmetry.
The scissors round a bend
behind a blushing ear.

And when the crime's done,
when the sun lies in its ashes,
a new child rises
out of the blond, unswept curls,
the suddenly serious chair
that last year was a roundabout.

All the way back to the car
a stranger picks himself out
in a glass-veiled identity parade.

Turning a corner
his hand slips from mine
like a final, forgotten strand
snipped from its lock.

Paul Henry

HIDE AND SEEK

You lose your father after dark
one Saturday, somewhere between
home and Singleton Park.

Huge cars roar past: you've never seen
shapes that black, eyes that bright.
Where will they go? Where have they been?

Your dad's nowhere in sight
and yet you never closed your eyes.
Now you are deep inside the night –

though night is only morning in disguise
– and every street light stares
at you, or soaks you in its dyes.

You're out alone, but no one cares ...
and then you hear the paws, the steamy breath
of wolves, of grizzly bears.

Stephen Knight

CRISS CROSS APPLE SAUCE

For Claudia

Criss cross apple sauce
do me a favor and get lost
while you're at it drop dead
then come back without a head
my daughter sings for me
when I ask her what she learned in school today
as we drive from her mother's house to mine.
She knows I like some things that rhyme.
She sings another she knows I like:
Trick or treat, trick or treat
give me something good to eat
If you don't I don't care
I'll put apples in your underwear ...
Apples in your underwear – I like that more
than Lautreamont's umbrella
on the operating table, I say to her
and ask if she sees the parallel.
She says no but she prefers the apples too.
Sitting on a bench
nothing to do
along come some boys - p.u., p.u., p.u.
my daughter sings,
my daughter with her buffalo-size heart,
my daughter brilliant and kind,
my daughter singing
as we drive from her mother's house to mine.

Thomas Lux

TWO FATHERS

The Good Father

If I had twenty children they would be
as neat and tidy as a gallery.
Though one might cry, another suck his thumb,
they need not fear the *Scissorman* to come;
nor *Boney*, nor the great *Agrippa*
could terrify these children with his slipper,
but each would be equipped with common sense
and every one replete with pounds and pence;
their dreams would stay in bed when they got up
to simple breakfasts and their own clean cup;
they'd have small bodies and enormous eyes
and all their sayings would be grave and wise.

The Bad Father

If I had twenty children they should slave
from morn till night, from cradle to the grave;
they'd go in rags and every night should shiver
to hear the *Banshee* howling for their liver;
their purses would be empty, their lives dull,
they'd feel their Master's knuckles on their skull,
Helen, Simon, Sophia, Michael, Thomas,
He'd teach them to be Enemies of promise;
They'd hide their heads when he knocked at the door
And when he could not find them he would roar:
You blocks, you stones, you worthless lumps of slurry,
Wait till I catch you, then you will be sorry!

George Szirtes

MAN OF STEEL

Superman is alive and well and living in South Brent.
I saw him this morning pushing a buggy with one hand,
pulling a stubborn toddler with the other, child and father
conjoined in a strange pas de deux in a stranger ballet.

He orders tea and an iced bun in Crumbs 'n' a Cuppa,
fills in the registration for his hour on the fourth plinth.
He's crucified by the bastard CSA, broke by Tuesday.
The money, at least, goes faster than a speeding bullet.

Some days he has to rip open his shirt to check he's still
himself, that red and yellow shield, the curled 'S'.
No-one wants a hero, so he's traded steel for satire,
subversion, and the slow collapse of his muscled belly.

These days he feels like the only man on planet Earth,
the only boy with a dad like Marlon Brando.
He crouches behind a cold chimney on a cold rooftop,
x-ray vision eyes burning with self-belief,

wraps his plastic cape of angel's wings around him,
planning a retcon, a re-boot, the comeback of all time,
and the Devon skies above him pulse with promise.
He does it all for Dean, aged four, and baby Billy.

Hilary Menos

KEEP THIS TO YOURSELF

There are country roads now that are empty.
They'll hold on to the light of the day
A bit longer, mindful some boy
May be heading home after a game.

Whoever he is, he'll have to hurry.
This lovely moment won't last long.
The road before him lies white
Here and there under the dark trees.

As if some mad girl in the neighborhood
Had emptied her linen closet
And had been spreading her things
Over the soft late-summer dust.

Charles Simic

FAMILY ALBUM

Loneliness – huge, suddenly menacing
and no one is left here who knows me anymore:
that Little League coach,
his TV repair truck and stinking cigars
and Saul the Butcherman
and the broken arm that fell out of the apple tree,
dead,
dead or gone south to die warm.

The little boy with mittens and dog
posing on the stoop –
he isn't me;
and the young couple in polo shirts, ready to pop
with their firstborn
four pages on in shortshorts and beatnik top
showing her figure off at 16...
1955 is in an attic bookcase
spine cracked and pages falling out.

Willow and plum tree
green pods from maple whirling down to the sidewalk...
Only the guy at the hot dog stand since when
maybe remembers me.
or at least looks twice.

But the smushfaced bus from New York dropping
them off at night along
these avenues of brick, somber as the dead child
and crimes of old mayors
lets off no one I know, or want to.

Warm grass and dragonflies –
O, my heart.

August Kleinzahler

MY SON ON CASTELL DINAS

Later, we walked up to the dinas holding hands.
Fosse, tump and cliff, erupted meeting place
of limestone and red sand,
grass sheepshitten, sheepcropped,
hawthorn and decaying fences.
Eastward, the track along the ridge
and all its folds of mountain falling north.
Westward, Mynydd Troed across the bwlch
hard and darkening in late afternoon.

The light plane towed a glider overhead
snorting in laborious air.
Its shadow rippled on the pant
and the gravel droning died.

Released from my hand, he ran
and played and made discoveries
and cairns and cromlechs
from the shale of fallen towers.

I saw grass and earth and stone
lichened, split, layered like the name –
castell – men in helmets holding natives down,
dinas – city before Rome breathed.
Cattle, slaves and iron bars.

A mile of air fell down towards the farms
blurring smoky in the shade.
Above the cup of land and ring of scarp,
high, the glider's lazy tilt and wheel
caught late sun on the wings,
glass teardrop of cockpit gleaming
pearly as aluminium.

He rampaged on the parapets
slipped from my reaching hand
cartooned to thirty yards of shadow.

I watched the ridge of Mynydd Troed turn black,
the towplane dropping in to shadow
trailing rope.

Christopher Meredith

COMEUPPANCE

I liked the way she said it,
like getting a fleck
of baccy off her lip:
You'll get your comeuppance.
It had a smack – more
than a smack – of inheritance,
the way she'd spit
those plosives out –
think *spite*, think *pittance*,
think *precious little* –
as I ducked outside
to pick a dandelion:
You'll get your comeuppance.
I took her word for it.

Her fear of dandelions!
We'd plant them in her slippers
or the cutlery drawer – ridiculous,
the way the littlest thing
betokened something –
her toothache, her bunions,
her illiterate faith in language –
the way an idle word,
a bitten-off breath,
could seed the day with auguries;
the way if you said *pig*
she wouldn't leave the house
but sit, fixed in her chair,
the way she sits today,

cast up on widowhood
like something brittle
while her daughters fuss about her.
Tight-lipped, she'll never speak
about their father. She'll die
asking if it's fair,
her fine-spun puff of hair –
flustered, pitiful,

backlit by the nightlight,
in the end
neither here nor there –
like a blown clock, or
yes, *Pittle-the-bed*,
as she might have said.

Paul Batchelor

THE POLICEMAN'S DAUGHTER

After Paula Rego

There she sits in her white dress,
all goodie-two-shoes, eyes downcast,
the little Miss Prim.

But she doesn't fool me
with all that elbow grease furiously
polishing his black boots at the kitchen table.

Look how her bare arm, fat as a ham,
disappears right down to the heel.
She'd have him believe she was a real

Daddy's girl. Twists him round her little
finger. But the set of her mouth, I know that.
The I-dare-you-to-tell clench of her jaw

when she pinches me under the gingham
cloth, sticks pins through the wings
of bluebottles she catches

in a sugar jar on the ledge of our attic
window, then fixes, as they squirm,
to her dress like shimmering brooches.

I've seen that flicker of a smile
curled at the corner of her lips
spread across her mouth like a kiss.

Sue Hubbard

HONEY

Away, away, he shouts, sending her up the hill,
through furze and bracken, to gather scattered sheep.
Listening for his whistle to bear left or right,
she snakes towards them, belly to the ground.

They raise their heads, sniff, ears pricked,
then flock together and run for the gate.
She comes back panting, stands at his side,
eyes bright, tongue lolling out.

She had the herding instinct from birth;
when she was just a pup he'd find her
in the haggard rounding up the hens.
You'll make a right cod of her, he gives out,

when we dress her up like our teacher
in our mother's headscarf and glasses.
We sit her at the kitchen table,
offer her a cup of tea and a scone.

A Sunday close to lambing, three men in the yard,
one with a rifle under his arm. *Your dog and Dunne's
wreaked havoc last night, thirty ewes dead or dying,
mangled in barbed wire, lamb beds hanging ou*t.

From an upstairs window we watch him
walk to the shed. He drags her by the scruff,
leaves her at their feet. He says nothing
when he comes in, says little for weeks.

Jane Clarke

THE CALL

for Brandon Etter

On this stretch of prairie,
seven hundred souls

with a particular awareness
of God.

The flat cast of the land
renders storms visible

from a great distance.
The flat cast of the land

is favoured by tornadoes
every spring and summer,

sometimes autumn.
In Stanford, Illinois,

no one calls the season
autumn. It is fall,

the whole year
could be fall,

hailstones, snowflakes,
the corrugated aluminium

of someone's roof.
There is a boy, nine,

who strains to see
beyond the horizon,

whose greatest wish
is a basement,

a cellar, 'the ideal place,'
the fireman said,

'to hide from tornadoes.'
Sometimes once,

sometimes seven times in a day
a grandfather's phone rings:

the boy wants to know
the weather,

its horrible plans.

Carrie Etter

RHODE ISLAND REDS

Haughty empresses of the byroad;
they scratch for grubs and worms
among dock and silverweed.

Back and forth they jerk their combs,
precisely splaying one wrinkled,
yellow foot in front of the other.

With flamenco flounces
they settle in dried-up puddles,
flick dust through their wings.

I remember the first time
I saw my mother choose one
and with deft wrist, wring its neck.

That night she plumped my pillows,
smoothed my sheets,
stroked the hair from my brow.

Jane Clarke

WHITEWASH

When I was maybe seven or eight years old,
I undertook to do a job for Nain
and paint the small backyard which used to hold
the bins, the coal shed and the washing line.
Although Nain's house has long been cleared away,
the grimy stones on next door's wall still show
the square of whitewash once as clean as day,
my handiwork from three decades ago.
And every time I walk up Tabor Hill,
I have to touch the patch of tarnished paint
to get a speck of proof that I am still
connected to a time that had no taint;
because for me there's nothing now at all
as pure as childhood's whitewash on the wall.

Grahame Davies

A FARMHOUSE NEAR MODENA, C.1980

O magnum mysterium

In the dark, the grey
Carrara shafts, with their scrolled
capitals.
        A small boy
sprung out of nowhere
charges in, gloves flapping
about his wrists.
He stops short.

Hay in the mangers, straw
on the bricked ground,
                        and white
oxen parted by the shafts –
freed from the yoke, patient,
heads to the wall,
gilt traces
tingeing their soft horns.

The boy standing among them
awed, a farmhand
stoops into the corner to lift out
for his gaze
a mother hedgehog suckling her eight young,
pinkish tadpoles dangling
from her teats.

Clive Wilmer

ON RETURNING A CHILD TO HER MOTHER AT THE NATURAL HISTORY MUSEUM

Hello my name is Kathryn and I've come
here to return your daughter, Emily.
She told me you'd suggested that she look
around upstairs in 'Earthquakes and Volcanos',
then meet you and her brothers in the shop.
You know that escalator leading to
the orb? It's very long and only goes
one way, you can't turn back. She asked me if
I knew the way back down and would we come
with her into the earthquake simulator –
that reproduction of the grocery shop
in Kobe, where you see the customers
get thrown around with Kirin beer and soy
sauce, things like that. She told us stuff about
your family. Apparently you had
a baby yesterday! That can't be right:
you're sitting here without one and my God
your stomach's flat! She also said she'd had
an operation in the hospital
while you were giving birth one floor below.
I know, I know: kids lie and get confused,
mine do that too. She talks a lot. She's fat.
She may not be an easy child to love.
I liked her, though. I liked her very much,
and having her was great, the only time
all day my daughter hasn't asked me for
a dog! We got downstairs and funnily
enough we found your middle son. He ran
to us upset and asked us where you were.
But here you are – exactly where you said –
the shop! Don't worry: I don't ever judge
a mother. Look at me: my daughter drank

the Calpol I left out when she was two;
I gave my kids Hundreds and Thousands once
for dinner while I lay down on the floor,
a wreck. I know you well! Here's Emily.

Kathryn Maris

A GRANDFATHER'S LAST LETTER

Elise, I have your valentine with the red shoes. I have
Waited too many weeks to write – wanting to describe
The excitement on the back lawn for you:
                                        the forsythia

Is now a bright yellow, and with the ribbons you draped
Inside it, trembles in a breeze,
All yellow and blues, like that pilot light this winter
Worried by just a little breath that came out of you.

On the dark side of the barn there's the usual railing
Of snow.
The tawny owl, nightingales, and moles
Have returned to the lawn again.

I have closed your grandmother's front rooms.

I know you miss her too. Her crocus bed showed its first
Green nose this morning. For breakfast I had
A duck's egg and muffins.

Your father thinks I shouldn't be alone?
Tell him I have planted a row of volunteer radishes.
I have replaced the north window ...

So you have read your first book. Sewed a dress for
The doll. The very young and old are best at finding
Little things to do. The world is jealous of us, you know?

The moles are busy too. Much more mature this year,
The boar with the black velvet coat made a twelve
Foot long gallery under the linden where the mockingbirds
Are nesting.

The moles took some of my rags to add to
Their nursery of grass, leaves, and roots.
The cream-colored sow is yet to make her appearance!
They have seven mounds. Each with three bolt doors

Or holes.
The pine martens are down from the woods, I see them
In the moonlight waiting for a kill.

Molehills can weaken a field so that a train
Passing through it sinks suddenly, the sleepers
In their berths sinking too!

I wonder what it's like in their underground rooms:
Their whiskers telegraphing the movements
Of earthworms. They don't require water when on
A steady diet of night crawlers. Worms are almost
Entirely made of water.

Last night there was quite an incident. The sun was going
Down and the silly boar was tunneling toward
The linden and he went shallow, the owl dropped down
Setting its claws into the lawn, actually taking hold
Of the blind mole, at that moment the mockingbird,
Thinking her nest threatened, fell on the owl putting
Her tiny talons into his shoulders. Well,

There they were, Elise, the owl on top of the invisible
Mole, the mockingbird on top of the owl. The mole
Moved backward a foot,
The birds were helpless and moved with him.
They formed quite a totem. The two birds looked so serious
In their predicament. A wind brushed the wash on the line.
And our three friends broke each for its respective zone.

Tomorrow the vines on the house are coming down. I want
The warmth of the sun on that wall. I'm sending
You a package with some of your grandmother's old clay
Dolls, silverware, and doilies.

Tell your father he is not coming in June to kill
The moles! Tell him to go fishing instead, or to take
Your mother to Florida.

You said you worry that someday I'll be dead also! Well,
Elise, of course, I will. I'll be hiding then from your world
Like our moles. They move through their tunnels
With a swimming motion. They don't know where they're going –

But they go.

There's more to this life than we know. If ever
You're sleeping in a train on the northern prairies
And everything sinks a little
But keeps on going, then, you've visited me in another world –

Where I am going.

Norman Dubie

MEGAN'S FIRST SNOW

Snow came floating through the black night,
your side of the channel, our side,
so here this morning
that dusting on our lawn has settled
in the corners of the garden,
crisp and tightening in the sun.

Not enough left now
to make a shroud or a marriage sheet,
but that patch beneath the privet
could be a gentleman's handkerchief.
Yes, I have decided, for us such token white
shall be *a gentlemen's handkerchief*,
our code for what remains of snow,
one of the things only you and I know.

Tony Curtis

LONDON

A full ginger moon hangs in the garden.
On this side of the house there are no stars.
When I go to bed, I like to soothe myself with
streetlights, lit windows and passing cars.

When my grandchild comes to sleep over
I find we share the same preference.
She doesn't want to draw the curtains either.
I like to look out on my town, my London...

Have you seen London from above? she asks me.
It's like a field of lights. And her grey eyes widen.
Her eight year old spirit is tender as blossom.
Be gentle to her now, ferocious London.

Elaine Feinstein

JEWELLED CARRIAGEWAY

We're on the way home, after my supper at Grandma's.
This is the stretch where my Mum can drive even faster
Because it is late and I'm already in my pyjamas.
I know that if I could bother to open my eyelids
I would see the various jewels: the dazzling diamonds
Approaching, the rubies falling more slowly back.

John Fuller

RIPPLES ON NEW GRASS

When all this is over, said the princess,
this bothersome Growing Up, I'll live with wild horses.
I want to race tumbleweed blowing down a canyon
in Wyoming, dip my muzzle in a mountain tarn.

I intend to learn the trails of Ishmael and Astarte
beyond blue ridges where no one can get me,
find a bird with a pearl in it, heavy as ten copper coins,
track the luminous red wind that brings thunder
and go where ripples on new grass shimmer
in a hidden valley only I shall know.

I want to see autumn swarms of Monarch butterflies,
saffron, primrose, honey-brown, blur sapphire skies
on their way to the Gulf. A gold skein
over the face of Ocean, calling all migrants home.

Ruth Padel

NOTES ON CONTRIBUTORS

Tony Curtis was born in Carmarthen in 1946. He is Emeritus Professor of Poetry at the University of Glamorgan where he established Creative Writing in the 1980s. He has published nine collections of poetry and has edited many books. His *Real South Pembrokeshire*, a personal response to that area, appeared in 2011. He is a Fellow of the Royal Society of Literature and a former chair of the Welsh Academy of Writers. www.tonycurtispoet.com

Daisy Goodwin is an award-winning British television producer, poetry curator and best-selling novelist. She was educated at Queen's College, London, Trinity College Cambridge and the Columbia Film School. Having joined the BBC as a trainee arts producer, she became Head of factual programmes at Talkback Productions before setting up Silver River Productions. Her first novel, *My Last Duchess*, was published in 2010; in addition Daisy has published eight best-selling poetry anthologies and a memoir entitled *Silver River*, and was chair of the judging panel for the 2010 Orange Prize for women's fiction.

Dannie Abse CBE was born in Cardiff in 1927 and trained as a doctor in London where he has lived since the war. His autobiographical novel *Ash on a Young Man's Sleeve* has been in print for over fifty years. He has published and edited many books, and his memoir of his wife late Joan, *The Presence*, won the Wales Book of the Year in 2008. *New Selected Poems 1949-2009* Hutchinson, 2009 was shortlisted for the Ted Hughes Award for New Work in Poetry and won the Wilfred Owen Poetry Award.

Alice Allen lives in London. She read English at Cambridge and then law. She is graduate of the M.Phil in Writing course at the University of Glamorgan.

Diana Barsham has taught at the University of Chichester and was for ten years Head of the English Department and a Reader in English at the University of Derby. She specializes in the literature of the nineteenth and twentieth centuries and has a special interest in Life Writing. Her major publications include books on Victorian Spiritualism and the Nineteenth Century Women's Movement (*The Trial of Woman* 1992) and a biographical study of the literary career of Sir Arthur Conan Doyle (*Arthur Conan Doyle & the Meaning of Masculinity* 2000).

Paul Batchelor was born in Northumberland. He works as a freelance writer and teacher. His first full-length collection of poems was *The Sinking Road* (Bloodaxe, 2008). He has received an Eric Gregory Award, the Arthur Welton Award, and the 2009 Times Stephen Spender Prize for Translation. www.paulbatchelor.co.uk.

Kate Bingham lives in London. Educated at Oxford, she is the author of two novels, *Mummy's Legs* and *Slipstream*. She is a recipient of an Eric Gregory Award and her poem 'On Highgate Hill' was nominated for the Forward Prize for Best Single Poem in 2010.

William Blake (1757-1827) was an artist and poet whose *Songs of Innocence* and *Songs of Experience* are some of the most profound and moving poems concerning childhood and the spiritual.

Alan Brownjohn was born in 1931 and has been publishing collections of poetry for over fifty years, most recently *Ludbroke and Others* from Enitharmon Press in 2010. He is also a novelist and editor. He was a member of The Group and is a Fellow of the Royal Society for Literature.

Marianne Burton's pamphlet *The Devil's Cut* (Smiths Knoll) was a Poetry Book Society Choice. Her work has appeared in places such as the *TLS*, *Poetry Daily*, and BBC Radio Four. Her first full collection is due this year from Seren.

Siobhan Campbell is the author of three poetry collections *Cross-Talk* (Seren), *The Permanent Wave* and *The Cold that Burns* (Blackstaff). Her chapbook *That Water Speaks in Tongues* was shortlisted for the Michael Marks Award and her work has won awards in the National, Troubadour and Wigtown poetry competitions. She lectures on the MFA in Creative Writing at Kingston University London and is the founder of the Military Writing Network there.

Gillian Clarke is currently the National Poet for Wales and one of the poets most widely read in the UK. She was awarded the Queen's Gold Medal for Poetry in 2010. www.gillianclarke.co.uk

Originally from a farm in the west of Ireland, **Jane Clarke** now lives in Wicklow. She is working on her first collection and has had poems published in *Envoi, The Stinging Fly, Southword, THE SHOp, Cyphers, Crannog, The Stony Thursday Book* and *Revival*. Jane has won a number of prizes and in 2009 was selected for the Poetry Ireland Introductions Series and was awarded an arts bursary. She has an Honours Degree in English and Philosophy from Trinity College, Dublin and is currently studying for an M.Phil in Writing at the University of Glamorgan, Wales. www.janeclarkepoetry.ie

Lynette Craig was brought up in Birmingham, read English and drama at Bangor, trained as a teacher and settled in London. When her children were small she started to write poems addressed to them. She was drawn to stories of her own and other Jewish families who came to the U.K. to escape persecution in Eastern Europe. This led to an interest in people forced to leave their homes: her themes are persecution, dispossession and the outsider. She also draws inspiration from the Bible, in particular from the stories of its women. Lynette, who holds an M.Phil from the

University of Glamorgan, conducts writing workshops for Exiled Writers Ink and The Jewish Museum in London. Her pamphlet collection, *Burning Palaces*, is published by Flarestack.

Grahame Davies is a poet, novelist, editor and literary critic, who has won numerous prizes, including the Wales Book of the Year Award. He is the author of 15 books in Welsh and English, including major studies of the Welsh relationship with Judaism and with Islam, and a novel about the French philosopher Simone Weil. His first volume of English poetry, *Lightning Under the Sea*, is published in 2011. His website is: www.grahamedavies.com

Jasmine Donahaye's books include *Whose People? Wales, Israel, Palestine* (University of Wales Press, 2012), and two collections of poetry: *Self-Portrait as Ruth* (Salt, 2009) which was longlisted for Wales Book of the Year), and *Misappropriations* (Parthian, 2006), which was shortlisted for the Jerwood Aldeburgh First Collection Prize. She has a BA from UC Berkeley and a PhD from Swansea University, and has published literary and cultural criticism, creative non-fiction and poetry in the UK and the US. She lives in mid-Wales.

Jane Draycott's new translation of the medieval dream-elegy *Pearl*, an extract from which was a Stephen Spender Prize-winner 2008, was published in 2011 by Carcanet/Oxford Poets. A Next Generation poet, and a previous winner of the Keats-Shelley Prize for Poetry, her collections include *The Night Tree* and *Prince Rupert's Drop* (short-listed for the Forward Poetry Prize) from Oxford Poets, and *Tideway* and *Christina the Astonishing* (with Lesley Saunders) from Two Rivers Press. Her most recent collection *Over* was shortlisted for the 2009 TS Eliot Prize. She teaches at the University of Oxford and Lancaster University.

Norman Dubie was born in Vermont in 1945 and is a graduate of Goddard College. He is the author of eighteen books and an outstanding narrative poet. He has received the Bess Hokin Award from the Modern Poetry Association and fellowships from the Guggenheim Foundation and the National Endowment for the Arts; his poetry has been translated into more than thirty laguages. He is Regents Professor of English in Arizona State University.

Carol Ann Duffy CBE, Fellow of the Royal Society of Literature, has been the Poet Laureate since 2009. Her latest collection, *The Bees*, was published in 2011.

Helen Dunmore is a novelist, poet, short-story and children's writer. Her work has received the Orange Prize for Fiction, the McKitterick Prize, the Nestlé Children's Book Prize Silver Medal and first prize in the National Poetry Competition; it has also been shortlisted for the TS Eliot Prize, the Orwell Prize and the Whitbread Novel Award, and longlisted for the Man

Booker Prize. A Fellow of the Royal Society of Literature, her books have been translated into twenty-eight languages. Her most recent novel is *The Betrayal* (2010).

Originally from Normal, Illinois, **Carrie Etter** lived in southern California before moving to England in 2001. She has published two collections, *The Tethers* (Seren, 2009), winner of the London New Poetry Award 2010, and *Divining for Starters* (Shearsman, 2011), and edited the anthology, *Infinite Difference: Other Poetries by UK Women Poets* (Shearsman, 2010). She is senior lecturer in creative writing at Bath Spa University. She blogs at carrieetter.blogspot.com

Vicki Feaver grew up in Nottingham "in a house of quarrelling women", an emotional inheritance which later found expression in her poetry. She studied Music at Durham University and English at University College, London and worked as a lecturer in English and Creative Writing at University College, Chichester, becoming Emeritus Professor. Her collections have been highly praised. The second, *The Handless Maiden*, includes the Arvon International Poetry Competition finalist 'Lily Pond', and 'Judith', which won the Forward Poetry Prize for Best Single Poem. The same collection was also given a Heinemann Prize and shortlisted for the Forward Prize, and she has received a Hawthornden Fellowship and a Cholmondeley Award. She currently lives in South Lanarkshire.

Elaine Feinstein was born in Liverpool, educated in Leicester, and read English at Newnham College, Cambridge, only a year after women were first admitted. She has written fifteen novels, and many radio plays and television dramas. Her work has been translated into most European languages. Her *Collected Poems and Translations* (2002) was a Poetry Book Society Special Commendation. In 1990, she received a Cholmondeley Award for Poetry, and was given an Honorary D.Litt from the University of Leicester. In 2005 she was awarded a Civil List pension in recognition of her services to Literature

Peter Finch is the former editor of *second aeon* magazine, manager of the Oriel Bookshop in Cardiff and CEO of Academi, now Literature Wales, the national development agency. He currently writes full time. His *Selected Later Poems* appeared from Seren in 2007 and *Zen Cymru* in 2010. He is currently writing *Edging the Estuary*, a book about the Severn Estuary. www.peterfinch.co.uk

John Fuller was born in 1937 and after a distinguished teaching career is now Fellow Emeritus at Magdalen College, Oxford. He has published fifteen collections of poetry, as well as novels and books for children. For twenty-five years he ran the Sycamore Press, publishing such poets as W.H. Auden, Philip Larkin and Peter Porter. He is a Fellow of the Royal Society of Literature.

Katy Giebenhain is the Poetry and Theology editor for *Seminary Ridge Review*. Her poems have appeared in *The London Magazine, The SHOp, Bordercrossing Berlin, Backbone Mountain Review* and other journals. A chapbook, *Pretending to be Italian*, is available from RockSaw Press. She lives in Pennsylvania and is a graduate of the Glamorgan M.Phil. course.

Roz Goddard is based in the West Midlands and works extensively as a writer in educational settings including schools, prisons and museums. Her most recent commission is for a series of poems linked to the George Shaw exhibition at the Herbert Art Gallery in Coventry. She has published four collections of poetry, most recently *The Sopranos Sonnets and Other Poems* (Nine Arches Press 2010).

Philip Gross is Professor of Creative Writing at Glamorgan University. He is a poet, writer of fiction for young people, science fiction, haiku and schools opera libretti, plays and radio short stories. His poetry up to and including the Whitbread Prize shortlisted *The Wasting Game* is collected in *Changes of Address* (2001) since when Bloodaxe have published four more collections. *The Water Table* (2009) won the TS Eliot Prize. A new collection, *Deep Field*, (2011) deals with his father's loss of language in old age. *I Spy Pinhole Eye*, with photographs by Simon Denison (Cinnamon 2009) was the English-language winner of Wales Book of The Year. His children's poetry includes *The All-Nite Café* which won the Signal Award, and *Off Road To Everywhere* (Salt, 2010) which won the CLPE Award for children's poetry. www.philipgross.co.uk

David Harsent's *Legion*, won the Forward Prize for best collection 2005. A new collection – *Night* – was published in 2011 and was shortlisted for the Forward Prize, the Costa Poetry Prize and the TS Eliot Prize.

Seamus Heaney was awarded the Nobel Prize for Literature in 1995. His most recent collection was *Human Chain* in 2010.

Paul Henry is one of Wales's leading poets. Described by U.A. Fanthorpe as "a poet's poet" who combines "a sense of the music of words with an endlessly inventive imagination", he came to poetry through songwriting. *The Brittle Sea, New & Selected Poems* has recently been published by Seren in the UK and by Dronequill in India, under the title *The Black Guitar*. www.paulhenrywales.co.uk

When **Lynne Hjelmgaard** was twenty years old she left her native New York city to live and study in Copenhagen, Denmark, where she married and had two children while studying at the Aarhus Art Academy and Frobel Seminarium in Copenhagen. After her husband's death she emigrated to England and presently lives in Brighton. Her first book *Manhattan Sonnets* was published with Redbeck Press in 2003. Her most recent, *The Ring* (Shearsman Books, 2011), is a response to being a new widow living in different European cities: Paris, London, Copenhagen and Rome.

Jeremy Hooker was born near Southampton in 1941, and educated at Southampton University. He has taught English and creative writing in universities in England, the Netherlands, the USA, and Wales, retiring as Professor of English at the University of Glamorgan in 2008. *The Cut of the Light: Poems 1965-2005* (Enitharmon, 2006) is a substantial selection from his ten volumes of poetry. His other books include *Welsh Journal* (Seren, 2001) and *Upstate: A North American Journal* (Shearsman, 2007), *Writers in a Landscape* (University of Wales Press, 1996) and *Imagining Wales: A View of Modern Welsh Writing in English* (University of Wales Press, 2001. He has edited selections of writing by Frances Bellerby, Richard Jefferies, Alun Lewis, Wilfred Owen and Edward Thomas. His website is www.jeremyhooker.co.uk

Sue Hubbard is a freelance art critic, novelist and poet. Twice winner of the London Writers competition she was the Poetry Society's first Public Art Poet and created a number of site-specific poems as part of a visual arts project in Birmingham's jewellery quarter. She was also commissioned by the Arts Council and the BFI to create London's biggest art poem that leads from Waterloo to the IMAX, and was writer-in-residence at the De La Warr Pavilion, Bexhill during ArchiTEXT week. Her first collection was *Everything Begins with the Skin* (Enitharmon 1994). *Ghost Station* was published by Salt in 2004.

Mary Husted was born in Leicester in 1944 and grew up in Sussex. From 1961 she studied graphics in Worthing but her studies were interrupted in January 1963 by the birth of her first son, Luke, who was given up for adoption. She returned to study graphics in Essen, Germany in 1963, but marriage and childrearing intervened – two marriages and four more children. In 1979 she moved to Barry, where she has been based ever since. As the children grew up she returned to writing and painting and went on to study Fine Art in Cardiff, graduating in 1990. Since then she has had solo shows in Wales, England, Canada, Hong Kong and Australia, as well as participating in group exhibitions in many countries. She has spent extensive periods living and working in Australasia. Her most recent solo exhibition, *Hush Don't Tell*, is a response to her lost son finding her.

Crystal Jeans was born in 1982 and lives in Cardiff. She is completing the creative writing M.Phil at the University of Glamorgan, where she writes both poetry and prose. Her pamphlet, *Just Like That*, was published by Mulfran Press in 2011. Most of the poems in the collection were influenced by her work as a carer for the elderly. She is currently working on a novel, a collection of short stories and a collection of poetry.

Mike Jenkins is a poet, fiction-writer and children's author, who lives in

Merthyr Tydfil. He is the winner of an Eric Gregory Award, Welsh Arts Council Young Writer's Prize, John Tripp Award for Spoken Poetry and Wales Book of the Year for his stories *Wanting To Belong* (Seren). A former editor of *Poetry Wales* he is co-founder and co-editor of *Red Poets*, an annual magazine of leftwing poetry. Now a full-time writer, who conducts many workshops, his latest book of poetry is *Moor Music* (Seren, 2010). He is a regular blogger – www.mikejenkins.net

Jackie Kay was born in Glasgow in 1961. She was adopted by a Scottish couple and brought up in that city. Her first book of poetry, the partially autobiographical *The Adoption Papers*, was published in 1991 and won the Saltire Society Prize; many other awards have followed including the Guardian First Book Award Fiction Prize for *Trumpet*, based on the life of American jazz musician Billy Tipton, born Dorothy Tipton. In 2010 she published *Red Dust Road*, an account of her search for her birth parents. Jackie Kay became an MBE in 2006.

Mimi Khalvati was born in Iran and grew up on the Isle of Wight. She trained at Drama Centre London and worked as an actor and director in Iran and the UK. She has published seven collections with Carcanet, including *The Meanest Flower* (2007), which was a Poetry Book Society Recommendation, a Financial Times Book of the Year and shortlisted for the TS Eliot Prize. Her most recent collection is *Child: New and Selected Poems 1991-2011*. Mimi is the founder of The Poetry School, where she teaches, and was the Co-ordinator from 1997-2004. She was poet in residence at the Royal Mail and has held fellowships with the Royal Literary Fund at City University, at the International Writing Program in Iowa and at the American School in London. Her awards include a Cholmondeley Award, a major Arts Council Award and she is a Fellow of the Royal Society of Literature. www.mimikhalvati.co.uk

August Kleinzahler was born in Jersey City in 1949 and now lives in San Francisco. He is the author of ten books of poetry and a memoir, *Cutty, One Rock*. His collection *The Strange Hours Travelers Keep* was awarded the 2004 Griffin Poetry Prize.

Stephen Knight was born in Swansea in 1960. He has published four collections of poems – *Flowering Limbs, Dream City Cinema, The Sandfields Baudelaire* and, for younger readers, *Sardines and Other Poems* – as well as a novel, *Mr Schnitzel*, which was the Wales Book of the Year in 2001.

Tom Lavelle lives and works in Galway, on the west coast of Ireland. His poems have been published in a wide range of Irish journals including *The Stony Thursday Book, The Cuirt Annual* and *THE SHOp*. He has been shortlisted in various competitions including Listowel Writer's Week 2010 and the Cork Literary Review Poetry Manuscript Competition in 2011. He was highly commended in The Over The Edge New Writer of the Year in both 2010 and 2011 and for the prestigious Patrick Kavanagh Poetry Prize in 2011. He is studying for an M.Phil in Writing at the University of Glamorgan and working towards a first collection.

Jenny Lewis is a poet, children's author, playwright, song writer and screenwriter. She has published two volumes of poetry, *When I Became an Amazon* (Iron Press 1996) and *Fathom* (Oxford Poets 2000) and her poems have been widely published. She has published three children's books, co-written a 26-part TV animation series (*James the Cat*) and her plays for children and young people have been staged at major UK theatres. Her verse drama, *After Gilgamesh* (Mulfran Press) premiered with music and dance at Pegasus Theatre, Oxford in 2011. She received a major grant from Arts Council South East for her next collection, *Taking Mesopotamia*.

Sarah Lindon's poems have appeared in *Magma* and *Seam*, and more are forthcoming in *Poetry Wales* and *Stand*. She is working towards an M.Phil in Writing at the University of Glamorgan, and lives and works in London.

Michael Longley was awarded the Queen's Medal for Poetry in 2001 and a C.B.E. in 2010. He was Professor of Poetry for Ireland from 2007 to 2010, a cross-border academic post set up in 1998. His most recent collection was *A Hundred Doors* (2011).

Thomas Lux was born in Northampton, Massachusetts in 1945, and taught at Goddard College, Vermont. His poetry books have won many awards including a Guggenheim fellowship, the National Endowment for the Arts and the 1995 Kingsley Tufts Poetry Award. He holds the Bourne chair in poetry at Georgia Institute of Technology.

Kathryn Maris was born in New York in 1971. She has a BA from Columbia University and an MA in creative writing from Boston University. Her first poetry collection, *The Book of Jobs*, was published in 2006, and her second will appear fom Seren in 2013. She has won a Pushcart Prize, an Academy of American Poets award, and fellowships from Yaddo and other artists' residencies. She lives in London and writes essays and reviews for *Time Out, Poetry London* and other journals.

Andrew McNeillie was born in north Wales and read English at Magdalen College, Oxford. He is the Literature Editor at Oxford University Press; in 2002 he established the Clutag Press to publish poetry. His collection of poems *Nevermore* (Carcanet, 2000) was shortlisted for the Forward Prize for Best First Collection. His collection *In Mortal Memory* was published by Carcanet in 2010. He has a chair in English at Exeter University.

Hilary Menos was born in Luton in 1964, studied PPE at Wadham College, Oxford and worked as a journalist and restaurant critic in London before moving to Devon to renovate a Domesday manor. Until

2011 she and her husband ran Beenleigh Manor Organics, a 100 acre organic farm breeding pedigree Red Ruby Devon cattle. Her first collection, *Berg* (Seren, 2009), won the Forward Prize for Best First Collection 2010. Her pamphlet *Wheelbarrow Farm* (Templar, 2010), was one of four winners of the Templar Poetry Pamphlet and Collection Competition 2010. www.hilarymenos.co.uk.

Christopher Meredith is a novelist, poet and translator. He was born in Tredegar, lives in Brecon, and has given readings and talks around the world. He has won an Eric Gregory Award, the Welsh Arts Council Fiction prize, and was shortlisted for the Welsh Book of the Year Award. His most recent poetry publication is the booklet *Black Mountains: Poems & Images* from the Bog-Mawnog Project (Mulfran, 2011). His fourth novel, *The Book of Idiots*, appears in 2012.

The adopted son of Irish and American parents, **Michael Murphy** (1965-2009) was born, grew up and lived in Liverpool for most of his life. Latterly he taught literature at Nottingham Trent University. *Proust and America* was published in 2008 and his *Collected Poems* appeared in 2011.

Kate Noakes lives in Caversham, Berks. She has degrees in Geography, and English Literature from Reading University and an M.Phil in Creative Writing from the University of Glamorgan. Her first collection *Ocean to Interior* was published in 2007 and a second, *The Wall Menders*, appeared in 2009. She is part of the performance group Brickwork Poets which gives themed readings around the country (www.brickworkpoets.co.uk). She blogs at www.boomslangpoetry.blogspot.com

Sean O'Brien is a poet, critic, broadcaster, anthologist and editor. He grew up in Hull and lives in Newcastle upon Tyne. He is Professor of Creative Writing at Newcastle University, Fellow of the Royal Society of Literature and 2007 recipient of the Northern Rock Foundation Writer's Award. His selected poems, *Cousin Coat: Selected Poems 1976-2001* was published in 2002 and his new verse version of Dante's *Inferno* in 2006. His first six poetry collections all won awards, most recently *The Drowned Book*, which won both the 2007 Forward and TS Eliot Prizes, the first time a book has won both awards. A book of short stories, *The Silence Room*, was published in 2008; *Afterlife*, his first novel, and *Night Train*, a collaboration with artist Birtley Aris, were published in 2009. His poetry collection *November* was shortlisted for the 2011 TS Eliot Prize and the Forward Prize. http://literature.britishcouncil.org/sean-obrien

Ruth Padel is Fellow of the Royal Society of Literature and of the Zoological Society of London, and Resident Writer at the Environment Institute and History Department, University College London. Four of her seven collections, most recently *Darwin: A Life in Poems*, have been short-listed for the T.S. Eliot and Costa prizes. She has also written an eclectic range of non-fiction, from studies of Greek tragedy to the influence of Greek myth on images of masculinity in rock music, and is highly acclaimed for her nature writing – in her novel, *Where the Serpent Lives*, and her eco-memoir *Tigers in Red Weather*. She has written three books on reading poetry: *52 Ways of Looking at a Poem*, *The Poem and the Journey* and *Silent Letters of the Alphabet*. Her new book *The Mara Crossing* mixes prose and poems on migration, both human and animal. www.ruthpadel.com

Geraldine Paine has an M.Phil in Writing from the University of Glamorgan. Her poems have been published widely in anthologies, and magazines. Her first collection, *The Go-Away-Bird* was published by Lapwing Publications (Belfast 2008). In an earlier life she was a professional actress, a specialist teacher and a magistrate. http://www.poetrypf.co.uk/geraldinepainepage.shtml

Don Paterson is an accomplished jazz musician and poet, which might partially account for the complex harmonies of his work. Born in Dundee, he left school to pursue a career in music, moving to London in 1984. At about this time he also began writing poetry. Stints in Brighton and Edinburgh followed as he developed his twin pursuits, forming the jazz-folk ensemble, Lammas, in the late 80s and publishing his first collection, *Nil Nil*, in 1993 which won the Forward Prize for the Best First Collection. Subsequent collections include *God's Gift to Women* and *Landing Light*, both recipients of the TS Eliot Prize. Paterson is currently poetry editor at Picador and teaches in the School of English at St Andrews University.

Mario Petrucci has been a schoolteacher, a physicist and ecologist, and is now a freelance writer and educator, a Royal Literary Fund Fellow, and has held residencies at the Imperial War Museum and with BBC Radio 3. Through the Poetry Society and the Poetry Library, he generates groundbreaking educational/writing resources combining poetry, science and ecology. His debut, *Shrapnel and Sheets* (Headland 1996), was a PBS Recommendation, while *Flowers of Sulphur* (Enitharmon 2007) won both the Arts Council Writers and New London Writers Awards. *Heavy Water: a poem for Chernobyl* (Enitharmon 2004) secured the Daily Telegraph/ Arvon Prize. *i tulips* (Enitharmon 2010) takes its name from Petrucci's vast Anglo-American sequence, of which *the waltz in my blood* (Waterloo 2011) is also part. Inspired by Black Mountain and the New York School, *i tulips* aims to reach 1111 poems. www.mariopetrucci.com

Pascale Petit's latest collection *What the Water Gave Me* (Seren 2010), was shortlisted for the TS Eliot Prize, Wales Book of the Year, and was a book of the year in the *Observer*. Petit trained at the Royal College of Art and spent the first part of her life as a visual artist before focussing on poetry. She has published five collections, two others of which, *The Huntress* and *The Zoo Father*, were also shortlisted for the TS Eliot Prize and were books of the year in the *TLS* and the *Independent*. She has been poetry editor at

Poetry London and was a co-founding tutor of The Poetry School. She currently tutors poetry courses for Tate Modern and is the Royal Literary Fund Fellow at the Courtauld Institute of Art. www.pascalepetit.co.uk

Sheenagh Pugh lived for many years in Wales, but now lives in Shetland. She has published many collections of poetry with Seren, including a *Selected Poems* and a *Later Selected Poems;* her most recent collection was *Long-Haul Travellers* (2008). She has also published two novels and a critical study of fan fiction, *The Democratic Genre* (Seren 2005). She has won the Forward Prize for best individual poem (1999), the Bridport and Cardiff International poetry competitions and has been shortlisted for the Whitbread and TS Eliot prizes.

Lynne Rees was born and grew up in Port Talbot, South Wales. Her poetry collection, *Learning How to Fall*, is published by Parthian, she is co-editor of *another country, haiku from Wales* (Gomer 2011) and she is currently researching and writing *Real Port Talbot*, forthcoming from Seren. She blogs as the hungry writer at www.lynnerees.com on life, food and writing.

Deryn Rees-Jones is the author of four collections of poetry and has edited for Bloodaxe an anthology of twentieth-century women's poetry. Her critical books include *Carol Ann Duffy* (1999, 2010) and *Consorting with Angels* (2005). Her forthcoming collection of poems from Seren is called *Burying the Wren.* She teaches literature at the University of Liverpool.

Jaime Robles is a native of San Francisco who lives now in Exeter. Her artist's books are in several special collections, at Yale, Berkeley and in Paris. Her most recent book was *Anime, Animus, Anima* (Shearsman 2010). These Foundlings poems were included in her chapbook *foundlings*, published in Exeter in 2011.

Born in London, **Sue Rose** lives in Kent and is a literary translator. She has an M.Phil in writing from Glamorgan University and her poetry has appeared in a variety of magazines and anthologies. She won the prestigious Troubadour Poetry Prize in 2009 and the Canterbury Poet of the Year in 2008. Her debut collection *From the Dark Room* was published by Cinnamon in September 2011. She is a founder member of Scatterlings, a group formed to give poetry readings in the Southeast and beyond. http://www.poetrypf.co.uk/suerosepage.shtml

Carol Rumens is visiting Professor of Creative Writing at Bangor University and the University of Hull. She was poetry editor for the *Quarto* (1982-4) and the *Literary Review* (1984-1988). She was elected a Fellow of the Royal Society of Literature in 1984, and has published many collections, most recently *De Chirico's Threads* (Seren 2010).

Lawrence Sail was born in 1942, educated at Oxford, and is a freelance writer. He was chairman of the Arvon Foundation from 1990 to 1994, has directed the Cheltenham Festival of Literature, was the UK jury member for the European Literature Prize (1994-96) and is a Fellow of the Royal Society of Literature. His most recent poetry collections are *Waking Dreams: New and Selected Poems* (2010), which draws on poems from ten previous collections, and *Sift* (2010) which is a memoir of childhood

Rosemary Shepperd is studying for a PhD at Glamorgan University. She was a finalist for the inaugural Manchester Poetry Prize and won 2009 the Ted Walters/ Liverpool University Poetry Prize. Her poems have appeared in magazines on both sides of the Atlantic and her Salt *New Voices* volume will be published later this year.

Charles Simic was born in 1938 in Belgrade and moved to the USA in 1954. He has published many collections of poems and translations. He became the fifteenth Poet Laureate at the Library of Congress in 2007 and won the Wallace Stevens Award in the same year.

George Szirtes's books include *Reel* (2004) which won the TS Eliot Prize, *New and Collected Poems* (2008) and *The Burning of the Books* (2009), shortlisted for the TS Eliot Prize. He has written fourteen books of poetry and translated or edited another fourteen of poetry and fiction from the Hungarian, as well as publishing an art monograph, a book of lectures, some libretti, and two books of poems for children. His next book of poetry is *Bad Machine* (Bloodaxe 2013). He teaches at the University of East Anglia, and is a Fellow of the RSL and of the English Association. www.georgeszirtes.co.uk

Victor Tapner has won several poetry prizes, including the Academi Cardiff International Competition and Scotland's Wigtown. His first collection, *Flatlands* (Salt 2010), traces 2,000 years of East England's prehistory, and won the poetry prize in the 2011 East Anglian Book Awards and has been shortlisted for the Seamus Heaney Centre Prize for Poetry. A former *Financial Times* journalist, he has an MA in Writing from the University of Glamorgan. Now a full-time writer, he lives in Essex. http://www.victortapner.com

Clive Wilmer was born in 1945. He teaches English at Cambridge and is also an Honorary Fellow of Anglia Ruskin University. He has published six books of poetry, including *Selected Poems* (1995) and *The Mystery of Things* (2006). His *New and Collected Poems* (Carcanet) appeared in 2011. He has edited the essays of Thom Gunn and Donald Davie and is working on an annotated edition of Gunn's *Selected Poems* for Faber. In 2005 he was awarded the Pro Cultura Hungarica medal for translation by the Hungarian Ministry of Culture for his translations of modern Hungarian poetry.

Samantha Wynne-Rhydderch has published two collections of poems, the latest of which, *Not in These Shoes* (Picador, 2008) was shortlisted for Wales Book of the Year 2009. Her work has been published in *Poetry Wales, Poetry London* and the *Independent* She has read at the Hay Festival, the Edinburgh Book Festival and the Ledbury Poetry Festival and received awards for her work from the Society of Authors (2007), the Hawthornden Foundation (2005) and the Academi Gymreig (1997 and 2002). Her next collection will be *Banjo* (Picador 2012).

Tamar Yoseloff is the author of four poetry collections, including *The City with Horns* (Salt 2011). She is also the author of *Marks*, a collaborative book with the artist Linda Karshan, and the editor of *A Room to Live In: A Kettle's Yard Anthology*. Two recent collaborations incorporating poetry and image, *Desire Paths* (with Linda Karshan and Galerie Hein Elferink) and *Formerly* (with Vici MacDonald) are published in 2012. She has run a number of site-specific writing workshops in venues such as Kettle's Yard, the Fitzwilliam Museum, Tate St Ives, and the Foundling Museum. She lives in London, where she is a freelance tutor in creative writing.

ACKNOWLEDGEMENTS

Dannie Abse. 'Child Drawing in a Hospital Bed' was first publsihed in *Arcadia One Mile* (Hutchinson 1998)

Paul Batchelor. 'Comeuppance' won the 2009 Edwin Morgan International Poetry Competition.

Kate Bingham. 'Crying' is taken from *Quicksand Beach* (Seren 2006).

Alan Brownjohn's 'Seven Activities for a Young Child' was collected in his *Collected Poems 1952-86* (Hutchinson 1988).

Gillian Clarke. Both poems are to be found in *Collected Poems* (Carcanet 1997).

Tony Curtis. 'Coram's Cloths' was published in 2011 as a Mulfran Press broadsheet.

Grahame Davies. 'The Mission Room' was translated as a group exercise at the Summer School of the British Centre for Literary Translation at University of East Anglia. 'Whitewash' was translated by the poet.

Jasmine Donahaye. 'Stillbirth' is from *Self-Portrait as Ruth* (Salt 2009).

Jane Draycott's version of *Pearl* was published by Carcanet in 2011.

Norman Dubie. 'A Grandfather's Last Letter' was published in *The Mercy Seat: Collected & News Poems 1967-2001* (Copper Canyon Press, 2001).

Carol Ann Duffy's 'A Child's Sleep' is from *Meeting Midnight* (Faber 1999).

Elaine Feinstein 'London' was first published in *Talking to the Dead* (Carcanet 2007).

Peter Finch's poem is taken from *Zen Cymru* (Seren 2010).

Roz Goddard. 'Rain' is collected in *Girls in the Dark* (Dagger Press 2002).

David Harsent. 'Blood Alley' is taken from *Night* (Faber 2011).

Seamus Heaney. 'Bye-Child' is to be found in Poems 1966-1972 (Faber 1973).

Paul Henry. 'Daylight Robbery first appeared in *Captive Audience* (Seren 1996).

Jeremy Hooker's poem is taken from *Our Lady of Europe* (Enitharmon, 1997).

Sue Hubbard. 'The Policeman's Daughter' was published in *Art World*.

Mike Jenkins' poem is from *Invisible Times* (Poetry Wales Press 1986).

Jackie Kay. 'Between the Dee and the Don' is from *Fiere* © 2011, Jackie Kay.

Mimi Khalvati's 'Picking Raspberries with Mowgli' is from *The Meanest*

Flower (Carcanet 2007)

August Kleinzahler. 'Family Album' is from *Rapid City: Poems New and Selected*, (Farrar, Straus, Giroux, 2008)

Stephen Knight's poems are from *Dream City Cinema* (Bloodaxe 1997).

Thomas Lux. 'Criss Crss Apple Sauce' appears in *New and Selected Poems: 1975–95* (Houghton Mifflin 1996).

Hilary Menos's 'Men of Steel' is from *Berg* (Seren 2009).

Christopher Meredith's poem is from *The Meaning of Flight* (Seren 2005).

Michael Murphy. 'Night Feed' is from Collected Poems (Shoestring Press, 2011).

Geraldine Paine. An earlier version of 'Still Life 1757' appeared in *The Go-Away-Bird* (Lapwing Publications 2008).

Don Paterson. 'The Circle' s published in *Rain* (Faber, 2009).

Pascale Petit. 'The Children's Asylum' is from *The Huntress* (Seren, 2005).

Jaime Roberts' poems are from her chapbook, *foundlings* (2011).

Lawrence Sail's 'Ghostings' is collected in *Waking Dreams: New and Selected Poems* (Bloodaxe Books, 2010).

Charles Simic. 'Keep this to Yourself' is from *Master of Disguises* (Houghton Mifflin Harcour, 2010).

Tamar Yoseloff. 'Tokens' is from *The City with Horns* (Salt 2011).